Developing the Interpreter;
Developing the Profession

Developing the Interpreter; Developing the Profession

Proceedings of the ASLI conference 2010

Edited by

Jules Dickinson & Christopher Stone

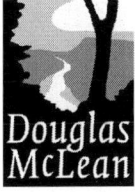

Douglas McLean Publishing
Coleford, Gloucestershire

First published in Great Britain
by Douglas McLean Publishing

© Association of Sign Language Interpreters 2012

This book is sold subject to the condition that they shall not, by way of trade or otherwise, be lent, re-sold, hired out or otherwise circulated without our prior consent in any form of binding or cover, other than that in which it is published and without a similar condition including this condition being imposed on the subsequent purchaser.
All rights reserved. No part of this publication may be reproduced, stored in a retrieval system, or transmitted in any form or by any means, electronic, mechanical, photocopying, recording or otherwise, without the prior written permission of the publisher.

ISBN 978-0-946252-79-4

Printed and Bound in Great Britain by
Print Academic, Exeter

Printed on recycled paper

Cover, layout and typesetting by
Douglas McLean

Douglas McLean Publishing
8 St John Street
Coleford
Gloucestershire
England
GL16 8AR

www.forestbookshop.com/mclean

Contents

Foreword.	7
Editors' notes.	9
Developing as an interpreter and seeing the profession develop. *Lorna Alsop*	11
The new challenge: Interpreting what was never said. *Anna-Lena Nilsson*	28
Do we agree on the roles, knowedge and skills set of Deaf interpreters? *Robert Adam*	39
Cultural Issues Within Deaf Visually Impaired Communication. *Barry-Alan Davey*	50
Clearing the Pathways to Success—Supporting and Developing New Interpreters. *Paul Belmonte and Jacqui Lees, Deaf Action*	61
Keep the balance—Holistic Stress Prevention. *Ralf Weibel*	77
'Well, it's green here, but I've seen green and green, and my mother's was always green': initial issues and insights from translating the BSL Corpus. *Kyra Pollitt, Janet Beck, Helen Dunipace, Sue Lee, Cathryn McShane, Elvire Roberts, Sherratt Rowan and Robert Skinner, and Adam Schembri and Graham H. Turner*	80
'Safe to Practice'—A holistic approach to interpreter assessment. *Maureen Saville & Stuart Anderson*	95
Professional recognition for Deaf interpreters in the UK. *Christopher Stone, John Walker & Paul Parsons*	109
I think you're my client, but you think you're my boss! *Helen Gillespie & Caron Wolfendon*	118

Foreword

It is a delightful privilege to introduce this collection of papers from what was an inspiring and thought-provoking conference of the Association of Sign Language Interpreters (ASLI) in Nottingham in 2010.

The conference proceedings includes a valuable range of reflections demonstrating the breadth of thinking and practice in the world of sign language interpreting at the present time.

Keynote papers begin this stimulating volume: Lorna Allsop of University of Bristol explores what it means for an interpreter to be a professional, including fascinating international, cultural and personal insights, then Anna-Lena Nilsson from Stockholm University tackles interpreters' vital and perpetual quest for meaning.

Cultural and practical issues continue in the papers from the presentations and workshops. Robert Adam engages us in a pertinent debate, seeking to find a way of defining the emerging group of professionals who are often called 'Deaf Interpreters'. Barry-Alan Davey examines interpreting from a perspective that is mindful of the culture of those people who are Deaf visually impaired. Paul Belmonte and Jacqui Lees look to those entering the profession and how we can ensure their success. Then those involved in the translation of the BSL Corpus offer some insight into the fascinating challenges this task required.

There is also focus on the constant striving of the sign language interpreting profession to uphold and raise standards.

Maureen Saville and Stuart Anderson discuss this from an assessment perspective. Christopher Stone, John Walker and Paul Parsons consider how the developing group of Deaf interpreting professionals in our midst are afforded recognition.

Further papers continue to reflect the importance of the well-being of individual practitioners, including Ralf Weibel's advice on stress prevention from a holistic perspective. Finally, Helen Gillespie and Caron Wolfenden remind us of the complex relationships between Deaf people working as professionals and the interpreters engaged alongside them.

Overall, these conference proceedings encapsulate an engaging and vibrant profession and pay tribute to the fascinating and stimulating thinking within the sign language interpreting community.

Thanks go to Doug McLean and Drs Jules Dickinson and Christopher Stone for their work in compiling and editing this volume.

Sarah Haynes
December 2011

Editors' Notes

Jules Dickinson & Christopher Stone

This volume brings together many of the contributions made at the ASLI conference 2010. The editors would like to thank the authors for engaging in a collaborative process enabling us to draw out the essence of their articles while trying to preserve the style of the individual.

The contributors represent the diversity of the members of our profession: academics, practitioner-researchers, practitioners as well as service providers and service users. This diversity also brings with it a variety of approaches and language uses when describing the professionals, communities and clients that we work with.

We the editors are aware of the debate regarding the use of Deaf or deaf to describe individuals with a hearing loss and understand the different perspectives of those advocating the use of capital D or lowercase d (see Atherton, 2005 and Napier, 2009 for a discussion of these issues). However, in this volume we have allowed individual authors to follow their individual sensibilities with regard to the use of deaf or Deaf. Similarly, we have taken no position with respect to the minimum length of the contribution nor its academic or practice focus. We hope you enjoy the conference proceedings.

References

Atherton, M. (2005) *Choosing to be deaf: leisure and sport in the British deaf community, 1945-1995*, PhD. thesis, Leicester: De Montfort University

Napier, J. (2009) 'Editorial: The Real Voyage of Discovery' *International Journal of Interpreter Education* 1, pp. 1-6

Developing as an interpreter and seeing the profession develop

Lorna Allsop

This paper is a written version of my keynote address, given at the ASLI conference in 2010, in relation to the theme 'Developing as an interpreter and seeing the profession develop.' The paper focuses on a number of considerations regarding International Sign (IS), its prevalence in training and its use in interpreting. I then consider, using a case study, the complexities of the relationship between Deaf and hearing interpreters when interpreting with IS. Finally, I refocus this discussion more broadly on issues of professionalism for Deaf and hearing interpreters as well as the dynamics of co-working for effective communication.

International Sign

My first 'international' experiences, as it were, mirror those of Deaf people around the world, i.e. through sports events or WFD meetings where one had the opportunity to socialise with people from different countries. At the time I gave little thought to the subtleties of the ways in which Deaf people were communicating or interacting with one another.

In 1985 I was invited to give a presentation to the first international workshop for deaf researchers hosted in Bristol, UK. I was asked to talk about my skills and knowledge in sign language teaching. I knew I would be presenting to a Deaf audience, all of whom could sign, and so I felt confident in accepting the invitation. It wasn't until the day arrived that it dawned on me that maybe I hadn't thought everything through in enough detail, and it wasn't going to be as easy as I had anticipated. The realisation that the audience came from many different countries from across the world was a cause for concern; how was I going to be able to get the ideas in my presentation across in a way that everyone could understand? At that moment it struck me that I knew nothing of other signed languages nor the vocabulary I would need for the presentation.

That was the beginning of the end for my presenting in other countries, as I refused any subsequent invitation that was made to me. The fundamental reason for my presenting was to share information and knowledge, and I could only do that if I was able to effectively communicate in a way that the audience would understand. As a result of that experience I began to reflect on how I could do this and actively started to observe other deaf presenters at international events.

Developing as an interpreter and seeing the profession develop

This single frame is taken from archive video footage of the workshops of ECDRSL (European Centre of Deaf Researchers of Sign Language), established in 1985. These workshops, held on a biannual basis, were attended by an international Deaf audience. The ECDRSL membership was exclusively Deaf, and sessions included topics such as linguistics, culture, the Deaf community, and psychology although this list is not exhaustive.

As Deaf people from different nations we did not have a shared sign language, and so had to find a way to communicate with one another. The image above shows Peter Jackson, a Deaf man from the UK. He is using BSL, but at a slower pace, utilising a larger signing space, and influenced by English syntax/grammar. This is a direct result of the Deaf person having to present the information for the first time in an academic setting, and wanting the audience to have access to the relevant jargon and terminology. The 'loud' clear mouthings (evident in the video footage) are also consistent with how a hearing person would articulate when communicating for the first time in a foreign country, i.e. foreigner talk.

The next photo is a single frame taken from footage of the

1991 workshop, hosted by Italy. The gentleman is from France, and is presenting on the topic of Deaf educators and the relevant lexical items required for teaching in this domain.

Initially, the impression from the video footage may be that the presenter is repeating himself. However, my interpretation is that he is striving to be understood, and therefore is constructing and expanding on a concept so that his audience is able to comprehend the point he is trying to make. He is taking time to create language structures so that his audience can visualize what he wants to express. In so doing he is using elements of French sign language (*Langue des Signes Française* or LSF), which is a beautiful and visually rich language, but at the same time, by being more 'international' in his sign he is also more cultural and inherently 'Deaf' in the way he presents his information. Rather than being influenced by the 'academic' setting, his priority throughout is for the audience to understand the message and context of his topic.

The process of how Deaf people from different nations can come together and negotiate a way to communicate is not something that spontaneously occurs without effort. The underlying (Deaf) value set and mode of communication (sign languages) may be shared, but it still requires careful consideration from the signer on how best to present the information. IS has developed through Deaf people coming together and creating a 'way' of communicating. The result is not 'one' fixed or established language, but instead there is a sense of fluidity in how IS strategies are used, with the language altering, dependant on who is using it, and where they are from.

I gained further insight and understanding of International Sign when working alongside Bencie Woll, Jon Martin Brauti and Senan Dunne on a research project. We explored whether IS was a language in its own right, comparable to other established and recognized sign languages (see Allsop, Woll and Brauti, 1995). This research confirmed my intuition that IS is not a language in its own right and that ideally Deaf people should be fighting for the training and provision of interpreters in their own languages, rather than for IS interpreting.

International Sign training for interpreters

Having introduced you to my understanding of IS, I want now to briefly discuss IS and interpreter training. As a result of other European funded projects, such as Horizon, interpreter-training initiatives were being developed and established across Europe, and I began to receive invitations (initially from Austria and Spain) to present information about IS. I was very reluctant to do so, as I was not convinced about the motivation behind interpreters of a signed language wanting to also become interpreters of IS. Additionally, I felt that the approach of this training was wrong. I realised, however, that the training would happen with or without my involvement, and so I accepted the invitation to mitigate the outcomes.

When presenting, I was explicit from the start about my

role. Whilst I was happy to talk about what IS was and how and why it was used, I was not there as a teacher. My stance originated from my belief that an interpreting student must first learn the sign language and culture of their country as completely as possible, before they can effectively use or understand IS. A further complication to the discussion is that IS is not a country specific language, so one would need to consider what this means for the 'culture' of IS and its use.

Whilst in Spain I not only worked with hearing interpreters, but also with a group of Deaf sign language teachers. It was interesting to note the contrast in attitudes between the Deaf and hearing groups. The Deaf group were only asking to be trained in response to hearing students demand to be taught; the hearing group were confident they could 'learn' IS with the sole aim of becoming IS interpreters. In reality the Deaf group were able to learn the principles with ease as they already had 'Deaf-native' knowledge of a signed language and of using visual/gestural communication with those who did not know their signed language.

This affirms my personal belief that those most equipped to learn and subsequently interpret IS are Deaf people; they already have a native and cultural understanding of a signed language, which they can then bring to bear upon using and understanding IS. I appreciate that some may disagree with my viewpoint and would reiterate my earlier statement that this paper is based on my personal experience.

Interpreting in International Sign—an example of good practice

With a clearer understanding of my views on IS, its use and its inappropriate placement in interpreter training, I would now like to move onto issues arising when interpreting in this domain. The following example describes some of the aspects of an assignment where I was required to work between BSL and IS, and will hopefully illustrate some elements of good practice. The event was a project management committee meeting, and there were two BSL/English interpreters present as co-workers, both of whom had experience working within international settings and who were familiar with the project. The spoken language of the meeting was English, with native speakers and second language learners present, some of whom had heavily accented speech. This caused comprehension problems for the BSL/English interpreters, as well as the interpreters working into spoken English from spoken and signed languages.

In analysing the situation it is worth thinking about the different elements present in the room. Firstly, I was there as a Deaf professional, but what did this mean? What were the affects of having delegates from many different countries? What was the impact of having so many different cultures in the room? Furthermore the meeting was chaired according to hearing norms and western conventions, and progress measured by speed and efficacy. We need to examine the affect I, as an interpreter, had on proceedings, including how I affected the power dynamic.

The interpreting team
Careful consideration was given to the layout of the room and the positioning of the interpreters, to ensure that it was conducive to both the British Deaf delegates and the French Deaf delegate. The interpreters alternated between simultaneous or consecutive interpreting, depending on the complexity of the information being interpreted. The interpreters had the challenge of processing complex information for their delegates, while also relaying the information for me to render into International Sign. It was crucial that we achieved a method

of co-working that allowed me to access the entire interpreted source message, and accommodated the process of effective translating between two visual modalities. I would watch a 'whole unit of meaning' and then transfer my eye-gaze to the Deaf delegate when producing my own (interpreted) signed message. This naturally meant I would miss the next section of information when I took my eyes off the interpreters, unless they changed to the consecutive mode.

There were many layers of interpreting happening at any one time, the spoken English source message was processed by an interpreter and translated into BSL; the next layer was me processing the BSL information and then translating into the target language (IS). This process incurred an extended time-lag that was intensified if I needed to stop the interpreters and ask them to clarify their message (they were not able to stop the source language, and even if they had it would be too far ahead by this time). I appreciate this method of stopping the interpreters so as to clarify their message may not be considered appropriate by some, but my priority was to ensure that the Deaf client accessed the information in full. For this to happen I needed to be clear in my understanding of the message before I could 'pass it on' to the French Deaf delegate. This may not be how 'hearing' BSL/English interpreters construct their role (NRCPD 2011), but should a Deaf interpreter comply with their culturally-bound role construction? It is an ethical question that I will explore a little later.

When the French Deaf delegate contributed to the meeting I would give myself time to ensure I understood the meaning of the signed message before translating it into BSL. I made a conscious decision that I could not provide a simultaneous interpretation, as I needed to maintain eye-gaze to comprehend the complete signed utterance. I would always search for meaning rather than just a direct sign-for-sign equivalent in the target language, whilst being mindful that this would then be re-interpreted into spoken English and so also needed to make sense culturally for the hearing people present (both interpreters and the delegates).

To make sure I had understood the original message I would interrupt the French Deaf delegate to ask for clarification as and when required. I also had to 'pause' the signed message to give me time to produce my BSL version. I used this 'consecutive' method as I had not received any preparation materials, and so had no prior knowledge to use as a point of reference. This method thus ensured greater accuracy.

Ethics and communication

Having considered some of the variables of the situation, I now wish to mention the interpreter's code of ethics or code of practice. Even though I may not have actively subscribed to the same interpretation of the rules for hearing BSL/English interpreters, I applied my own 'Deaf' value set to the way I felt I should work. I believe it was important to establish a working relationship with the Deaf delegate, in order to ensure we could communicate effectively. I felt it was my responsibility to ensure the message could be delivered to all parties. After the meeting ended I took time to converse with the Deaf delegates, to ask how they felt about the interpretation of the meeting. I also wanted to acknowledge my awareness of my presence in the interaction, and my affect on the fluidity of the information as I interrupted Deaf delegates and the other interpreters. This extended to the British Deaf contingent. as their experience of the BSL/English interpreting provision was also affected.

For me, the important thing was the feedback from the Deaf delegates. They stated that they were satisfied and happy with my work, which I believe can be attributed to the degree to which I was honest and transparent about the situation

I was in. It was appreciated that I was precise about what I was interpreting and could request specific elements of the utterance that needed clarification. I showed awareness of the environment and my affect on it. The Deaf delegates felt they retained the control, as they were reassured that my process was acting in their best interests. Maybe it was clear from the way I conducted myself that even when interpreting I am a Deaf person first and foremost, and a 'professional' second. Professionalism as it is currently interpreted can be a barrier for Deaf people (see Allsop 2007); a 'professional' presence becomes problematic as opposed to the 'communicative' presence many Deaf people desire.

A useful analogy can be drawn upon with TV documentaries. If you are watching a TV programme about a tribe in Africa or the Amazon, the presenter (who may be a researcher or an explorer) would be non-native to the environment and so would have a local 'fixer' to guide them through the culture of the tribe, and act as interpreter. This person would become the intermediary between the outsider and the tribe. So how does this person behave? Do they follow a set of ethics? Which countries' ethics do they use (the British visitors' or the tribes)? They are acting as an interpreter to give access to the visitor, but also to help them achieve what they need to gain from their experience with the tribe. The visitor is reliant on the guide to relay the questions they ask, to interpret the responses, to probe deeper into the culture that informs the answers.

This also highlights the (occasional) issue that arises regarding 'ownership' of the interpreter by the Deaf person. As an interpreter you often feel that you are impartial and so are acting for both the Deaf and hearing people equally in any transaction. However the perspective of some Deaf people is that you have learnt and are using their language for your career, and so this places an additional responsibility on the interpreter to be an ally.

The idea of the Deaf person 'owning' the interpreter can create tensions and misunderstandings if an interpreter is not aware of Deaf peoples' culture and history, or what it means to be a member of a minority group. Sign language cannot be separated from the culture of the Deaf people who use it; sign language can only occur if Deaf people come together and so they own it. If an interpreter only learns the language but does not take on board the culture that accompanies it then they are missing a key component of any interaction and this will affect the way they communicate with, and interpret for, Deaf people. And this issue has become more widespread since the rise of the interpreter as a 'professional'.

Issues of professionalism and effective communication

The IS context described above, interpreter training and working within a team of Deaf and hearing interpreters gives you some of my insights into interpreting, Deaf and hearing interpreters working together, and effective communication with Deaf clients. This section will now address the profession of interpreting and what this means in terms of expectations, both of the individual and ethical. I will also consider the ways in which Deaf people and interpreters work together and the power relations that can be at play.

The professionalisation of interpreting in the UK

In my lifetime I have seen many changes in the function, definition and role of an interpreter. Having grown up in a Deaf family, when interacting with hearing people in an everyday setting I would write things down. By the 1960s the missioners were at their most prominent and they would help to interpret situations between Deaf and hearing people, such as translating telephone calls or at interviews (see Corfmat, 1990). In the 1970s, changes in support structures for Deaf people in the field of social care meant that Deaf people had more regular support from a social worker, who would deal with everyday interaction on their behalf (Scott-Gibson, 1991). At this time it was common for Deaf people to ask other Deaf people who had more advanced language skills to act as a language broker in interactions with the hearing community (Adam et al, 2011). Within the work place hearing colleagues have been relied on to interpret for Deaf staff, assisting them with telephone calls etc. From my personal experience, hearing work colleagues have voiced over for me when I have presented a paper at conferences. This was a practical arrangement as we worked alongside one another and they had background knowledge of my work. In a Deaf club setting the principle was often a CODA[1] or a hearing person, who had worked with the Deaf community and was competent at using sign language, and would work as an interpreter for Deaf people. Once formal training programmes were established for interpreters there was a significant period of change, as hearing people with no previous knowledge of or contact with the Deaf community could undertake training to become an interpreter. This was the start of the control being taken from the Deaf community in terms of interpreting (see Allsop and Stone, 2007).

As Deaf people have gained a greater understanding of the role and responsibilities of an interpreter, they have begun to aspire to this role as a career option. I always encourage them to do so, but have noted than many have commented thay they feel they cannot 'meet' the requirements of being an interpreter. I feel they may be referring to the code of ethics

---

[1] Child of Deaf Adult(s)

and conduct that hearing interpreters are required to adhere to. The codes were created, informed and constructed by hearing people. Whilst they are also principles that a Deaf person can refer to, I would suggest that there are some differences between how they would be interpreted and practised by Deaf interpreters. The question we may need to ask is what makes a professional in this context? What is their role and responsibility? I suggest that there are four underlying principles for all interpreters to follow:

- Make sure they are clear so that all parties understand what is happening
- Be careful not to create an adverse affect for any of the participants present
- Show respect to all involved and to the situation
- Treat all participants as equals

I believe that this set of behaviours defines the person as a 'professional', rather than the setting or environment they are working within.

Co-working and effective communication

Interpreters are guided to actively work for a period of 20–30 minutes, then 'break' or swap with a co-worker. This way of working is understandable; the process of interpreting between two languages is mentally tiring. Sustaining a certain level of effective processing for longer periods is hard to achieve, and therefore co-working allows the interpreting to continue, and for the level of processing to be managed (Moser-Mercer, Künzli and Korac, 1998). The interpreting process is commonly understood—one takes from a source language (spoken or signed) the meaning or intent and a suitable translation is rendered in the target language (spoken or signed). When co-working, the interpreter will hand over to a co-worker after their allocated time is up and 'rest'. This is a process proffered by the interpreting team and has little engagement with the Deaf client.

Whilst Deaf interpreters also use this model, different considerations are brought to bear on the interpreting situation. For Deaf interpreters there is increased interaction and a continuous bond with Deaf clients. This is not only because both parties are Deaf, but because the modality in which both the interpreter and the client receive and produce information is always visual. A non-active hearing interpreter can listen to the speaker and be relatively passive, only needing to become a 'visual participant' when actively rendering into signed language. The resting Deaf interpreter however is always receiving information visually. The Deaf interpreter is not able to 'rest' per se, as it would be culturally inappropriate for them to 'look-away' from the Deaf client. They cannot completely disengage from the interaction, and thus cannot take a break in the same way as hearing interpreters. There is a continued element of processing during this time that differs from hearing interpreter colleagues; Deaf interpreters have to process the information given and consider the cultural aspects and context in which the information is given, over and above processing between two languages (and modalities).

When interpreters, Deaf and hearing, are working in a team it is crucial that they support each other in every element of the work; to each share cultural and linguistic knowledge enabling the other to function better; to teach one another about cultural norms in a Deaf or hearing context; to help overcome problems that arise during an assignment; to make sure the Deaf client is satisfied with the provision they are given. *Looking On* (Young, Ackerman & Kyle, 2002: 24) reported that 'the open exchange of opinions between deaf and hearing colleagues was considered a vital factor in creating positive working relationships.' In other words, from the Deaf person's point of view, being consulted about their opinion by hearing people was clear evidence that both they and their views were valued and respected. The elicitation of the opinions and views of Deaf people demonstrates that the Deaf perspective matters and can be influential, and that in situations where hearing people tend to occupy the senior positions of responsibility, power and the decision making, it 'is an important means of equalising power relationships.'

The dynamics of working in a Deaf and hearing interpreter team need to be addressed, as often the domain and assignment is biased towards the hearing interpreter, for example the chair person of a meeting will often greet the interpreters in spoken English. Preparation materials and documentation is in written English, therefore the dominant language and culture benefits the hearing interpreter in the first instance. This is not the fault of the interpreter, but it is something that needs to be recognised and discussed openly, so that strategies can be found to allow both Deaf and hearing interpreters to be equal.

Conclusion

For me, Deaf people becoming professionally recognised as interpreters is a positive move. And I feel that hearing interpreters should embrace these newer members into the profession. Working alongside a Deaf interpreter gives hearing interpreters insights into how Deaf people communicate with one another not only on a linguistic level, but more importantly on a cultural level too. Until now, Deaf people have not been able to register at the same level as hearing interpreters but this does not mean they should have had a lesser status. Whilst they may not interpret the code of ethics in the same way as their hearing colleagues, it does not mean that they are not ethical or that they are not working as professionals. As a Deaf interpreter with IS experience I believe that as Deaf interpreters we understand the code from our own cultural rules, and strive for behaviours that ensure equity for Deaf clients and effective communication.

References

Allsop L, 2007 Interpreter From A Deaf View, MSc Dissertation (unpublished),

Allsop L and Stone C, Collective notions of quality in interpreting: insights from the British Deaf Community, at SASLI 25th anniversary conference, 5th and 6th October 2007, Edinburgh, Scotland.

Allsop, Woll and Brauti,1990 *Bilingualism and International Sign*, S.Prillwitz(ed) Proceedings of the Fourth European Symposium on Sign Language Research, Hamburg: Signum Press

Corfmat, Percy. 1990. *Please sign here: insights into the world of the Deaf* (Vol. 5). Worthing and Folkestone: Churchman Publishing.

NRCPD 2011 http://www.nrcpd.org.uk/documents/reg_docs/bsl_english_interpreters/bsl_eng_code_of_ethics.pdf [accessed July 2011]

Scott-Gibson, L. 1991. Sign Language Interpreting: An Emerging Profession. In *Constructing Deafness*, ed. S. Gregory and G. M. Hartley, 253–58. London: Pinter in association with the Open University.

Moser-Mercer B, Künzli A, Korac M. 1998 . Prolonged turns in interpreting: Effects on quality, physiological and psychological stress (Pilot study) Source: *Interpreting, Volume 3, Number 1*, pp. 47–64(18) Publisher: John Benjamins Publishing Company

Young AM, Ackerman J, Kyle JG. 2002. *Looking On: Deaf People and the Organisation of Services* (2nd Ed). Bristol.

The new challenge: Interpreting what was never said.[1]
An eternal question and a new explanation

Anna-Lena Nilsson

One of the motivating forces behind both this presentation, and the PhD thesis I recently finished, is also one of the eternal questions of interpreting: 'Who is doing what, and to whom?' Strangely enough, this key aspect of what somebody is saying is frequently misinterpreted by sign language interpreters. For a long time I have been interested in trying to find some possible reasons for this being so.

In this paper we will look at a new way of describing how signed languages express who is doing what to whom. This, in turn, helps explain the challenge in the title of this presentation—as sign language interpreters we are expected to interpret not only what is said, but also what is *not* said. To be fair, what is new is not the challenge of interpreting what was never said, but rather the insight that this is what we do. Since sign language interpreters mainly work between one spoken and one signed language, we will also take a look at differences between spoken and signed languages. Possibly,

---

[1] This presentation is based on a paper presented at the EFSLI 2010 Conference in Glasgow, 11 September 2010, and on Nilsson (2010).

part of the reason that information is misinterpreted can be found in differences between these two modes of communication.

Differences between spoken and signed languages

Many spoken languages rely on word order as a key component in signalling who is doing what to whom. In English, for example, if you say '*The dog bit the postman*' that means something completely different from saying '*The postman bit the dog*' even though the exact same words are used. In addition, even in those spoken languages that do not rely as heavily on word order, the language is in itself sequential, in the sense that words are produced one after the other. Thus, even though certain aspects of meaning can be expressed using for example intonation, it is not physically possible to produce two spoken words at the same time.

If we now turn to signed languages, they do have an equivalent to word order, in that signs can be produced one after the other. There are grammatical, as well as ungrammatical, ways of producing strings of signs, where the order the signs are produced in decides whether the string of signs is grammatical or not. However, as opposed to spoken words, more signs than one can be produced at the same time, while also co-occuring with other linguistic signals. This means several aspects of meaning can be produced simultaneously. In addition, a signer can also use the three dimensional space around him/her in different linguistically meaningful ways. Signs can be meaningfully directed in signing space, and the signer can move his/her body while producing them. This linguistic use of space is particular to signed languages, and has therefore been of key interest in signed language research through the years. Some of the concepts that have been used to describe these aspects particular to signed languages are for example 'role shift', 'role taking', and 'placement'.

In previous research, a prescriptive view of reference in signed languages has been prevalent. According to this view, to produce a sequence of signs using 'role shift', a signer must first introduce a referent, and 'place' or 'locate' the referent somewhere in signing space. Only when this has been done is it possible to 'take on the role' of that referent.

The idea that a referent must first be identified, and then placed somewhere, was the basis also for descriptions of pointing signs used for reference. That is, to use a pronominal pointing sign produced in a certain direction to refer to a specific entity, that entity first had to be identified with lexical signs and 'located' in that direction.[2]

The meaning of words and signs

According to a view of language and communication that has informed much previous research as well as interpreter training, meaning is found 'inside' words or signs. That is, words and signs have a meaning attached to them — there is something that they always mean. If we regard language and communication in this manner, then the interpreter's task is simply to decode the meaning of each word or sign produced in the source language, and then recode it in the target language. In other words, as sign language interpreters all we have to do is to interpret what is said.

However, we only need to consider a word such as *bed*, to realize that words do not have one fixed meaning. Upon hearing that word, most of you will probably think of a bed like the one you have in your bedroom. However, there is (at least) one more kind of bed—the *flower bed*. Therefore, the meaning of *bed* depends on the context where the word is used. To describe how we know exactly which referent the speaker has in mind in a certain context, the concept of 'frame'

---

2 A short summary of previous research regarding this can be found in Nilsson (2008).

(Fillmore, [1982] 2006) has been used. As Fillmore defines it, a frame is a system of concepts '…related in such a way that to understand any one of them you have to understand the whole structure in which it fits; when one of the things in such a structure is introduced into a text, or into a conversation, all of the others are automatically made available.' (2006: 373)

This frame concept can help explain that knowing, for example, that the context of an event is a garden exhibition evokes a 'gardening frame', which in turn makes it easier to identify *bed* as a *flower bed* in that situation, and not a bed you sleep in. Thinking along these lines will be of importance when we consider the fact that interpreters are expected to interpret not only the inherent meaning of the words that are used, what is said, but what the words actually mean in a certain context.

Cognitive Linguistics

According to a more recent view of language and communication known as Cognitive Linguistics, meaning is not something that resides in words or signs, meaning is something that is constructed by the speaker and the addressee together.[3]

According to this way of describing language and communication, interpreters are co-constructors of meaning. As sign language interpreters, we are not the primary addressees of what the speaker/signer is saying. However, we also have to construct meaning from what is said, and we then produce our rendition of it in another language.

Based in Cognitive Linguistics, Wilcox & Shaffer claim that '[m]eaning is not conveyed in form. Meaning is inferred from, constructed on the basis of, form' (2005:35). Here, 'form' refers to the linguistic form, that is, to signs or words. What they are saying is that the signs and words used do not convey meaning in and of themselves. Signs and words are

---

3 Readers interested in this theoretical framework can find more details, as well as further references, in Nilsson (2010).

only the basis on which we build to construct meaning when we communicate.

According to Wilcox & Shaffer, this way of describing language and communication also influences our view of interpreters. It gives '[t]he picture /.../ of an active interpreter, not one with direct access to the meanings and intentions of others, but of a maker of meaning on the basis of the cues provided by others.' (2005:47)

Recent research on signed languages supports this view of language and communication as an activity where people construct meaning together. Analyzing a dialogue in Norwegian Sign Language, Liddell & Vogt-Svendsen come to the following conclusion:

'Thus, contrary to the widely accepted (prescriptive) view that signers must identify every spatial element prior to making use of it, we find that this signer provides explicit identification of only some of the elements of her real space blends. The conceptual task of creating the remainder of each real space blends [sic!] falls on the addressee.' (2007:193)

As we will now see, similar results are also found in Nilsson (2010).

Example from Swedish Sign Language[4]

In the Swedish Sign Language discourse from which this example was taken, the signer has previously discussed patients who know they are dying from cancer, and used meaningfully directed signs to indicate an area in front of her to be used for that referent. She later returns to talking about these dying persons with the signs glossed in (1), and thereby sets up a new scenario:

---

4 The following discussion is based on one of the examples analyzed in Nilsson (2008, 2010) where it is described in detail. A discussion of some theory specific concepts used, such as 'surrogate blend', 'THEME-buoy', etc. can also be found there.

(1)[5]   #IF SAY ONE PATIENT cl-PERSON>|dying person-forward|
        THEME-buoy----------------
        PATIENT cl-PERSON>|dying person-forward| DYING touch-THEME-buoy

'If, for example, you have a patient who is dying…'

During the re-introduction of the dying persons in (1), the signer's gaze alternates between looking at the area in front of her that was previously used for that referent and looking at the addressee. As she touches the THEME-buoy produced with her non-dominant (left) hand (cf. the last gloss in (1)), she nods her head, then turns slightly to the right and looks forward/up (seen in the first photo in Figure 1). She has now 'taken on a role', which in cognitive linguistics' terms is described as 'having created a surrogate blend', where she herself represents such a dying person.

Knowing that s/he is soon about to die, this dying person demands to meet somebody, to talk, now. COME-HERE>|left/up| is directed to the left and upward, thus creating an 'invisible surrogate' for the somebody whom the dying person wants to talk to, located to the left of the signer. The signer thereby creates a spatial contrast (right–left), which helps the addressee separate out the referents. The verb DISCUSS is also produced to the left and upward (indicated by the superscript >|somebody|), and the signer as the dying person looks up to the left, as if talking to that invisible somebody. Note, however, that we are never explicitly told that there is a person located up to the left, nor who that person is.

Next, a comment from narrator's perspective is inserted (#NOW NON-1ST-SING>|dying person-forward| WANT, 'That's what s/he would want.'), seen in the third row in Figure 1. Here, the

---

[5] Brief glossing conventions are found after the reference section, whereas details regarding the glossing can be found in Nilsson (2008).

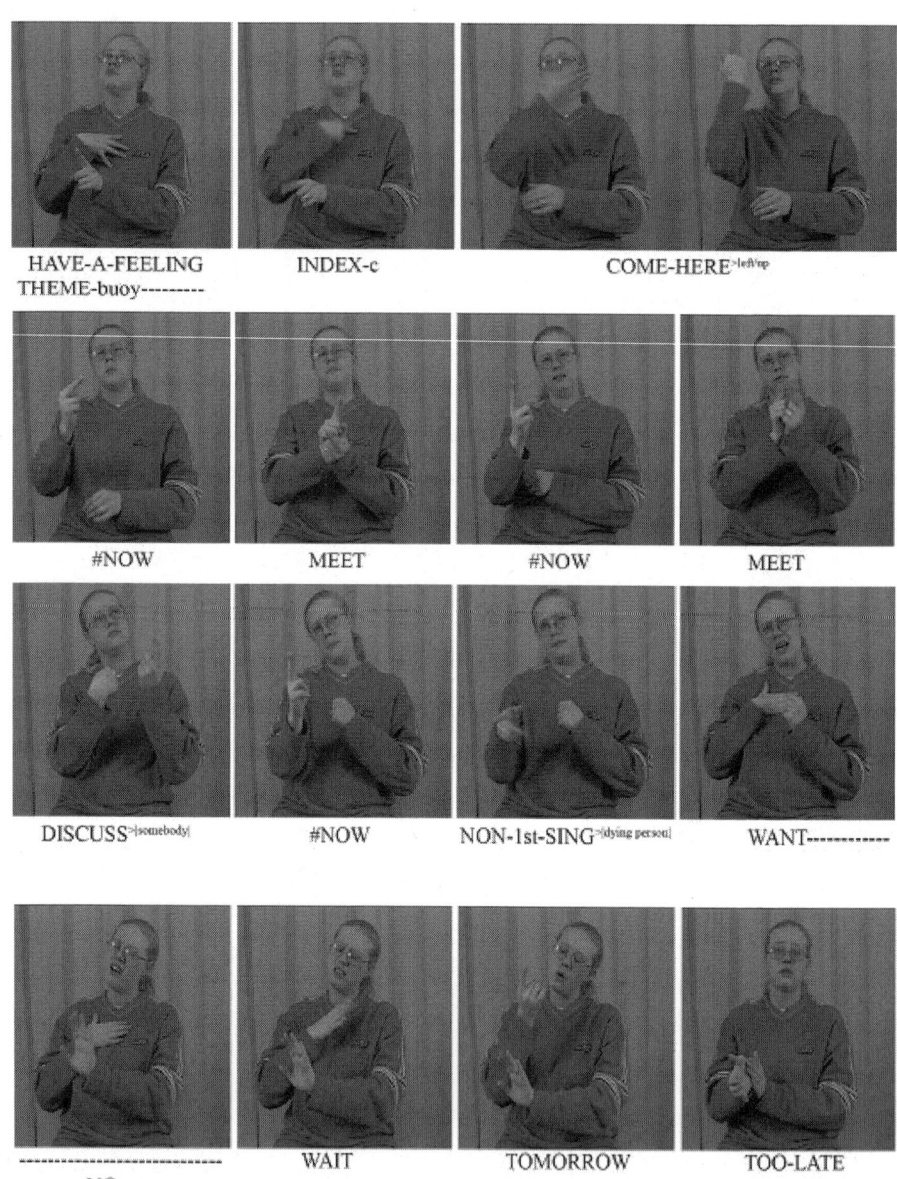

Figure 1: ... 'who has that feeling [that s/he will soon die], and demands to meet somebody to talk now. That's what s/he would want. Then you mustn't say "No wait till tomorrow." Because then it would be too late.

signer returns to being the narrator, and directs the pronominal pointing sign NON-1st-SING towards the area in front of her which has previously been used for that referent, while her gaze is directed at the addressee. Note also that the signer's head is tilted to the right here.

During the following signs, NO WAIT TOMORROW (the first three photos in the last row), the signer suddenly tilts her head slightly to the left instead, thus creating a new surrogate blend. The signer does not state explicitly 'whose role she now takes on', or in the terms used in cognitive linguistics: which person she now 'blends with, creating a new surrogate blend'. We can deduce that it is somebody who is in a position to say *no* to the request from the dying person, and since the current frame is one of health care, it is likely to be a member of hospital staff. In this blend, the signer produces a sequence with 'constructed dialogue', using the signs NO WAIT TOMORROW ('No, wait until tomorrow.'). The complex sequence in Figure 1 ends with a one-sign comment, where the signer returns to narrator's perspective again (TOO-LATE).

How do we understand, and interpret, what was never said?

We have now seen that there are indeed times when the signer does not identify a referent before 'taking on the role' of that referent. Moreover, we have seen that the signer does not tell us the identity of a referent 'located' at a place that signs are directed toward, either. This means that not all referents are explicitly identified by the signer. The question we then have to ask ourselves is: What knowledge do we, as addressees and/or interpreters, need in order to understand what the signer is saying, and thereby to know 'who is doing what to whom'?

In the chapter by Liddell & Vogt-Svendsen (2007) mentioned above, they discuss the kinds of knowledge the speaker and the addressee in the analyzed dialogue use to 'build similar Real Space blends' (that is, to conceptualize signing space similarly). They use their shared knowledge of the world, as well as their shared knowledge of the current discourse. As the conversation moves along, they keep constructing meaning together, and making sure they understand each other. To do this, they also need shared knowledge of the grammar of the language they are communicating in. An additional source of knowledge that is particular to signed languages, is that they use information from the directional signs produced by the signer.

Concluding remarks

As we have seen, meaning is not a fixed part of a word or sign, but something that is jointly constructed in context by the speaker/signer and the addressee. This kind of meaning construction is central to people understanding each other. In order to construct meaning of what people are saying/signing, interpreters need a good command of their working languages. In addition, interpreters need broad general knowledge that can help us construct meaning in the many different contexts where we are interpreting.

Not even this is enough, though. If we are to acquire the specific knowledge needed to construct the appropriate meaning in a certain situation, we have to be given a chance to prepare for specific assignments. This in turn means that speakers need to be ready to share their world(s) with us. If they do, we can conceptualize space the way they do, and construct the same meaning they do, which we can then produce in another language—thereby interpreting also what was never explicitly said.

References

Fillmore, Charles J. 'Frame semantics.' in *Cognitive Linguistics: Basic Readings.* edited by Dirk Geeraerts (Berlin: Mouton de Gruyter, 2006.) 373–400. Originally published in Linguistic society of Korea (ed.) *Linguistics in the Morning Calm.* (Seoul: Hanshin Publishing Company, 1982.) 111–137.

Liddell, Scott K., and Vogt-Svendsen, Marit. 'Constructing spatial conceptualizations from limited input: evidence from Norwegian Sign Language.', in *Gesture and the Dynamic Dimension of Language. Essays in Honor of David McNeill. Gesture Studies 1.,* edited by Susan D. Duncan, Justine Cassell, and Elena T. Levy (Amsterdam/Philadelphia: John Benjamins Publishing Company, 2007), 173–194.

Nilsson, Anna-Lena. *Spatial Strategies in Descriptive Discourse: Use of Signing Space in Swedish Sign Language.* CDS/CLCS Monograph Number 2, Series Editor: Lorraine Leeson. (Drumcondra, Ireland: Centre for Deaf Studies, University of Dublin Trinity College, 2008) 80 pp. *http://su.diva-portal.org/smash/record.jsf?searchId=1&pid=diva2:305811&rvn=19*

Nilsson, Anna-Lena. 'Real Space blends in Swedish Sign Language as an indicator of discourse complexity in relation to interpreting.' In Nilsson, Anna-Lena, *Studies in Swedish Sign Language. Reference, Real Space Blending, and Interpretation.* (Stockholm: Stockholm University, 2010) 85 pp. *http://su.diva-portal.org/smash/record.jsf?searchId=1&pid=diva2:305811&rvn=19*

Wilcox, Sherman, and Shaffer, Barbara. 'Towards a cognitive model of interpreting.' in *Topics in Signed Language Interpreting: Theory and Practice.* edited by Terry Janzen (Amsterdam/Philadelphia: John Benjamins Publishing Company, 2005), 27–50.

Glossing conventions in brief

Where two lines are used, the upper line contains glosses for signs produced with the signer's dominant (right) hand, and the lower line contains glosses for signs produced with the signer's non-dominant (left) hand. A line of hyphens (---) is used to indicate the duration of a sign, when that is of particular interest.

SAY	Words in small caps represent signs.
#IF	Words in small caps preceded by a '#' represent fingerspelling.
cl-PERSON	A noun classifier.
NON-1st-SING	A non-first person singular pronoun.
>left/up	'>' indicates that a sign is meaningfully directed, and can be followed by either the direction used, or by a description of the mental space entity the sign is directed toward.
THEME-buoy	A sign produced with the signer's non-dominant hand.

Do we agree on the roles, knowledge and skills set of Deaf interpreters?

Robert Adam
Research Associate
Deafness Cognition and Language Research Centre
University College London

Introduction:

The purpose of this presentation was to look at the roles, knowledge and skills set of Deaf interpreters (referred to as DIs in this article as there are a number of BSL signs and English terms which cover the various aspects of a DI's work). It has become increasingly obvious there are differing perspectives on what indeed a DI is, ranging from a DI being an assistant to a non-Deaf interpreter, to a DI being a professional in his or her own right. These differing perspectives are of some concern because they often arise from a lack of knowledge and understanding of DIs and the sort of work a DI does. This is also of concern because a simplistic analysis of DIs may have an adverse impact on the recognition and the place of this work within the interpreting profession. To understand the work of a DI it makes sense to examine the various roles, knowledge and skills set of DI, in order to define this field of work. It is hoped that in clarifying this, we will have a better understanding of what a DI does, and thus foster better working relationships between Deaf and non-Deaf interpreters, both within and outside of interpreting assignments.

Research to date:
Ladd (2003) refers to the minority language group we call the Deaf community as a collective community, where Deaf people have traditionally supported each other through various ways, including an exchange of manual skills. Deaf people have traditionally been trained and employed in the manual trades. Deaf people who were good at carpentry for example would support other Deaf people who have other skills such as repairing motor cars or cobbling shoes or tailoring (Ladd, 2003). This skills exchange has not been confined to just the manual trades as Deaf people have also helped each other with written and signed translations of various texts (Stone, 2006). In fact this is not only within the Deaf Club—a number of researchers (Boudreault, 2005, Stone, 2009, Adam, et al. 2011) all refer to Deaf children interpreting for classmates in the classroom where the classroom teacher is not able to understand or make themselves understood by their Deaf pupils. This indicates that what Deaf people do in the Deaf club often originates in school.

This raises the question of what exactly is done? Often this included translation and the drafting of letters and documents by bilingual Deaf people. Adam, et al. (2011) found that bilingual Deaf people were often also committee members (quite often Secretary or Minutes Secretary) of Deaf clubs/groups using their bilingual skills to support their minority language community; as members of the community they garnered trust from within the Deaf community. There is a little researched or known about various aspects of DI 'work' to date, as it is community internal, highlighting the fact that non-Deaf people are not the only ones who have done this kind of language brokering within the Deaf community.

DIs—a new concept?

Boudreault (2005) has the following two quotes in his seminal chapter on Deaf interpreters, the first one being a question posed to a Deaf interpreter: 'How can a Deaf person be a sign language interpreter in your own Deaf community? It can't be. You're Deaf!' (Boudreault, 2005:323) and yet he reports that: 'There is a new trend around the world for the Deaf interpreter service provider to be an integral part of Deaf life' (Ibid.). This lack of consistency is also evident in the UK where DIs have their legitimacy questioned.[1] And yet the work of a DI is not new—for as long as Deaf people have communicated with each other using sign language, Deaf people have also acted as language brokers. Carty et al. (2009) tells the story of a Deaf woman, Sarah Pratt of Weymouth, Massachussets, born in 1640, whose Deaf husband with the help of her two sisters, wrote down her replies to the elders of her church as a part of her examination for membership of the congregation. It is reasonable to assume that although this is the first documented evidence that for as long as Deaf people have been coming together as a community there have been Deaf members of that community who have been DIs.

Terminology:

Another area where there does not seem to be any consistency is the terminology used to describe DIs. They are in addition to 'deaf interpreters', variously called 'relay interpreters', 'deaf relay interpreters', 'intermediaries', 'mirror interpreters', etc. Napier et al. (2006) defines relay interpreting: being an 'intermediary communicator between a non-Deaf interpreter and a deaf client, a deaf presenter and

---

[1] See also Morgan and Adam, (submitted) for a discussion of Deaf interpreters' experience in working with non-Deaf interpreters, as well as with agencies/non-Deaf clients who do not understand the work done by Deaf interpreters.

a deafblind client, or a non-Deaf interpreter and a deafblind client' (see also Bienvenu and Colonomos, 1990). On the other hand, Boudreault (2005) uses the term Deaf interpreters, but states that they were sometimes assumed to be 'language facilitators' or a 'mirroring' interpreter. Forestal (2005) refers to intermediary interpreters, with the non-Deaf interpreter remaining the lead interpreter in any given situation. Adam et al. (2011) refer to Ghostwriters, who are Deaf people performing translation tasks for other Deaf people, acting as language brokers for people in a community where not everyone has English as a strong second language.

It is of interest to note that some of the terminology (for example, relay interpreters, intermediary interpreter, mirror interpreters) used can be taken to meant that DIs exist only to assist the non-Deaf interpreter, and other terminology (DI) seems to indicate that Deaf interpreters are in a professional field of work which is quite distinct from but closely associated with non-Deaf sign language interpreters. It is proposed therefore that 'Deaf Interpreters' (DIs) be used to cover the range of work that is done, which will be discussed in the next section.

So what is a Deaf interpreter?

As discussed, there are a number of different perspectives on what a Deaf interpreter is. Napier et al. (2006) state that Deaf interpreters are assigned when the client: uses own signs or home signs; uses a foreign sign language; is Deafblind or has limited vision, uses signs particular to a region, ethnic or age group that are not known to the non-Deaf interpreter; or is in a mental state that makes ordinary interpreted conversation difficult. This definition is useful in looking at some of the situations in which a Deaf interpreter can work. Boudreault (2005) on the other hand presents a concise description of the different aspects of Deaf interpreting work; the various language situations a Deaf interpreter is booked to work requires: a Deaf bilingual with skills in a spoken and a signed language; Deaf people who work between two sign languages; and Deaf people who work within one sign language (i.e. Deaf interpreter mirroring, working as a facilitator, working with Deafblind people). This is particularly useful especially in the context of the UK where, anecdotally, Deaf people who work within one language do most of their work.

Yet some researchers (Collins and Walker, 2005) refer to the first and second group and do not consider the third group (i.e. Deaf people who work within one sign language) as Deaf interpreting work. I would argue that as most DIs do this form of work in one way or another sooner or later in their professional work, that this is an integral part of DI work, and that DIs who are skilled at inter-language work are usually able to do intra-language work and vice versa. Because of obligations under the Broadcasting Act (1996) and the Communications Act (2003) there exists a pool of DIs who work from English to BSL on television, which makes it somewhat easier to argue that DI work is exclusively inter-language. However, there is similar anecdotal evidence that intra-language work forms a considerable proportion of the work done by DIs in the UK.

What is the difference between a DI and a non-Deaf interpreter?

Discussions with workshop participants in Prague (EFSLI spring school, 2010) and the ASLI Conference in Nottingham (2010) resulted in the following lists of similarities between DI and non-Deaf interpreters:

Similarities:

- bilingual (minimum requirement)
- processing (language, whether inter- or intra-lingual still needs to be processed)
- code of conduct
- professionalism
- roles
- work

Differences:

- DIs are Deaf all the time (i.e. non-Deaf can go home)
- access to information
- culture ownership; confidence with culture
- links with Deaf community; role model
- code of conduct
- nuances of situation
- acceptance and recognition
- speech is not a central part of interpreting
- role of advocacy

Of interest is the point that the code of ethics was similar and yet different for both groups. It was argued that because of the different cultural starting points of DI and non-Deaf interpreters, that the code of ethics, while equally applicable to both groups, would have different implications for each. Additionally, the role of advocacy was discussed; although it was agreed that DIs are not advocates, because of DIs' different cultural standpoint there is a perceived difference in how Deaf clients are supported in different situations. For example, DIs will pragmatically enrich and/or impoverish the message in different ways from non-Deaf interpreters (Stone, 2009).

When are DIs assigned?

An earlier view of DIs (Egnatovich, 1999:1) was that non-Deaf interpreters thought: 'certified Deaf interpreters are only there for deaf people with minimal language skills or whenever I need them'. However Bienvenu and Colonomos (1992) in discussing the role of DIs conclude that while it is difficult for non-Deaf interpreters 'to admit that a relay interpreter is necessary', this is not a sign of a weak interpreter, but rather, 'a disciplined and ethical interpreter.' Some situations call for the use of two qualified interpreters—it's as simple as that.' DIs are necessary for a number of reasons (Forestal, 2005):

> . . . when required by law, particularly in legal and medical settings, in serious matters, including mental health, sychiatric and drug/alcohol treatment programmes, public events, and when the non-Deaf interpreter is not qualified, due to the great demand for interpreters, sometimes the non-Deaf interpreter is not quite ready to actually interpret. There are other domains, such as Deaf-blind people, international events.

Attitudes have moved on from then, and workshops (EFSLI summer school, 2010 and ASLI conference 2010) have examined the potential situations in which a DI is assigned:

> Where there is a barrier
> Written translation
> When another Deaf person is needed
> TV translation and interpretation
> Media settings
> Mental health settings
> Child protection
> Arrest
> Immigration
> Teaching
> Significant life events such as weddings and funerals.

With respect to the work actually done by a DI—it is indeed varied: it can include voicing, gesturing, writing or using other sign languages (Boudreault, 2005, Adam et al. 2011).

Deaf Extralinguistic Knowledge:
A working document of the National Consortium of Interpreter Education Centers[2] refers to the knowledge gained through these first-hand Deaf world experiences as Deaf Extralinguistic Knowledge, or DELK, which is a prerequisite to training as a DI and is:

> . . . needed in consumer assessment, message analysis, even in the production phase of the interpreting process, to achieve an interpretation that is consistent with the linguistic and experiential frame of the deaf consumer. (2009:1)

The same document refers to the formative experiences of a Deaf interpreter which include (2009:2):

1.1.1. Exposure to American Sign Language and a wide variety of other communication forms of deaf people through life-long interactions with Deaf family members, Deaf peers within the education system, and Deaf people in the community.
1.1.2 Early experiences of interpreting for family and peers;
1.1.3 Experiences of personal challenges to comprehending situations, interpreters, and various communication styles;
1.1.4 Personal experiences of discrimination, oppression, and what it is like not to have access to communication.

This discussion paper neatly dovetails with some of the findings of Adam et al. (2011) who discuss traditional DIs who have had a life-long experiences of ghostwriting and language brokering within the Deaf community.

---

[2] http://media.ncrtm.org/presentations/SShop/DIDOMAINS.pdf

Conclusion

While there have been differing views of what DI is, this paper argues that a Deaf interpreter is defined as a Deaf professional who does both inter- and intra- language interpreting as well as translation from English to sign language. There is a different cultural standpoint for DIs and non-Deaf interpreters, and this has implications for some aspects of DIs' work, particularly with respect to the code of ethics and how the message is rendered. Finally, the partnership of DIs and non-Deaf interpreters will lead to an increase in service delivery standards for Deaf people.

Acknowledgement:

The support of the Economic and Social Research Council (ESRC) is gratefully acknowledged. Robert Adam was supported by the ESRC Deafness Cognition and Language Research Centre (DCAL) Grant RES-620-28-0002.

References:

Adam, Robert., Breda Carty, and Christopher Stone. 2011. *Ghost writing: Deaf translators within the Deaf Community.* Babel. 57 (3).

Bienvenu, MJ., & Betty Colonomos. 1992. "Relay interpreting in the 90s." *The Challenge of the 90s: New Standards in Interpreter Education, Proceedings of the Eighth National Convention of the Conference of Interpreter Trainers*, Laurie Swabey (ed.), 69–80. United States: Conference of Interpreter Trainers.

Boudreault, Patrick. 2005. "Deaf interpreters". *Topics in Signed Language Interpreting: Theory and Practice*, Terry Jantzen (ed.), 323–355. Philadelphia: John Benjamins.

Carty, Breda, Susannah Macready, and Edna Edith Sayers. 2009 *"A Grave and Gracious Woman": Deaf people and Signed Language in Colonial New England.* Sign Language Studies, 9: 297-323.

Collins, Judith. & John Walker., 2006 Deaf Interpreter, What is it? in *Proceedings of the Inaugural Conference of the World Association of Sign Language Interpreters, Worcester, South Africa. October 31st–November 2nd 2005.* Edited by Locker McKee, R. Douglas Mclean Publishing.

Egnatovitch, Reginald. 1999. Certified Deaf Interpreter—WHY? RID *Views*, 16: 10.

Forestal, Eileen. 2005. The emerging professionals: Deaf interpreters and their views and experiences on training. *Sign Language Interpreting and Interpreter Education: Directions for Research and Practice.* Marc Marschark, Rico Peterson & Elizabeth A. Winston (eds.), 235–258. New York: Oxford University Press.

Ladd, Paddy. 2003. *Understanding Deaf Culture: In search of Deafhood*, Clevedon: Multilingual Matters.

Morgan, Pamela, and Robert Adam. 2012. Deaf interpreters in mental health settings—some reflections and thoughts for Deaf interpreter education. *Examining the Education of Healthcare Interpreters.* Karen Malcolm and Laurie Swabey (eds.). Washington, D.C. : Gallaudet University Press,

Napier, Jemina, Rachel McKee, and Della Goswell. 2006. *Sign language interpreting: Theory and practice in Australia and New Zealand.* Sydney: The Federation Press.

Stone, Christopher. (2009). *Towards a Deaf Translation Norm.* Washington: Gallaudet University Press. .

Websites:
http://media.ncrtm.org/presentations/SShop/DIDOMAINS.pdf (accessed 31 July 2011)

Cultural Issues Within Deaf Visually Impaired Communication

Barry-Alan Davey

Introduction

The aim of this paper is to share some of the things I have learnt about the culture of Deaf visually impaired people (Deaf VI people) and the way they use language. This in turn will provide insights into what interpreters need to know, do, and understand about Deaf VI people's language and culture, thus enabling us to provide a more holistic service to the Deaf community.

Some background information

I have worked with Deaf VI people for about nine years. My experience with this group of people began at the age of eighteen, when I was employed as an RNID community support worker. I worked with Deaf adults with additional needs such as mental health, physical disabilities and vision loss. During this time I was a key worker for a Deaf person who had a significant sight loss, and who used 'Hands-On' communication. Having never undertaken any sort of 'Deafblind' communication before, I was a little lost when first presented with what seemed like a daunting task. However, I was fortunate that person was very understanding and patient: working with him was an invaluable learning experience.

My subsequent work as a freelance communication support worker and a communicator/guide for Deaf VI people gave me a much wider perspective on the needs of Deaf VI people, from both a communicational aspect as well as cultural comprehension. This dual perspective is necessary in order to properly understand the differences between 'standard' Deaf culture and Deaf VI people's language use. The biggest culture shock came when I had been in the job for about two years, when I met someone who showed me more about Deaf VI culture than I ever would have learnt on my own. As someone with Usher syndrome, over the last four years this person has shown me both the big and small differences between Deaf and Deaf visual impairment, differences that I would never have noticed had I never met her.

The Culture of Deaf VI People

The term Deafblind is an umbrella term, categorising anyone with a dual sensory loss. Language is unequivocally linked to culture and as Kramsch (1998:3) states, 'language is the principle means whereby we conduct our social lives. When it is used in context of communication, it is bound up with culture in multiple and complex ways'. Members of the Deaf community have their own culture and mannerisms because of their language. Likewise, Deafblind people have their own culture and language.

Image 1 (overleaf) shows the front cover of the highest level

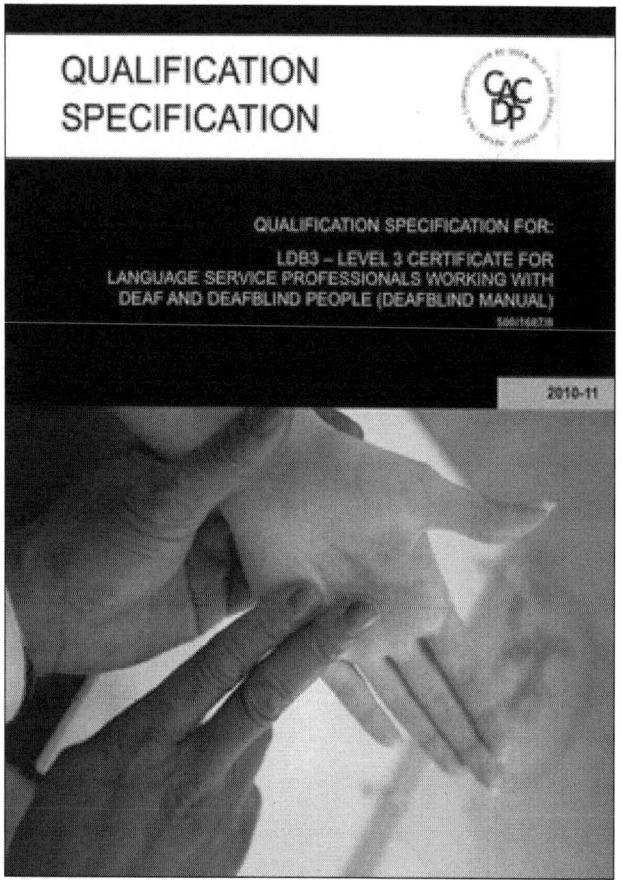

of qualifications linked to the Deafblind communication method, 'Communication tactics for Deafblind people'.

Deaf people with a visual impairment consider themselves as (and are by any definition) 'Deaf'. That is to say they have a Deaf identity, culture and language, they have Deaf friends, partners and/or Deaf family, and they communicate using British Sign Language (BSL). They are therefore in many ways just like the 'regular' BSL users that interpreters work with on a daily basis. However, because Deaf VI people are unable to communicate using sign language visually, I would suggest that many members of this community feel as though their needs are often overlooked.

'Deaf VI' does not solely describe people with Usher syndrome, but can account for anyone who is culturally Deaf with a visual impairment. In this category therefore we can include people who have lost their sight through accident, illness or any other way, e.g. glaucoma, rubella, cataracts, brain damage, stroke and detached retinas. There are hundreds of different eye conditions that can cause severe visual impairment and according to the British Society for Mental Health and Deafness (2010) Deaf people are, 'nearly five times more likely to have a Visual Impairment, nine per cent compared to two per cent [in the general population]'.

To meet their communication needs Deaf people can request a BSL interpreter. From the enquiries I have made with some of my contacts in the Deaf VI community, it seems that getting an appropriate level of service from a BSL interpreter is problematic. If a Deaf VI person requires an interpreter they are presented with two options on the booking form: Deafblind (manual) or BSL (visual). Unless a Deaf VI person specifically asks for an interpreter who is used to providing 'Visual Frame' or 'Hands-On' interpreting, they will not receive this type of communication support.

Although there are interpreting qualifications for Deafblind manual and BSL, there appears to be very little recognition of the communication methods used by Deaf VI people: Visual Frame and Hands-On. These are both communication methods which adapt BSL to meet the needs of those people who cannot receive this language through the standard visual method. Interpreters, as language professionals, need to know the best methods to adapt the way they use language in order to meet the needs of Deaf VI people. The following sections outline some of the ways in which interpreters can make these adaptations.

Practical adaptations

I was not formally taught any of the adaptations or methods discussed in this article, but instead I have I learnt to adjust my communication through conversing with Deaf VI people themselves. They have taught me to sign in ways that enable understanding, along with my own reflective practice, which is one skill that has been particularly beneficial. My long-standing relationships with a large number of Deaf VI people have led to many opportunities to work in this field. After every Hands-On and Visual Frame assignment I reflect on what went well, what difficulties occurred and how I overcame them. This means that if the same challenges arise again, I am able to address them more effectively. In the section below I will outline the main adaptations, however, I would emphasise that in my view the best way to learn is to 'do'.

Visual Frame

Visual Frame is signing within a person's limited or restricted field of vision. This may be used, for example, if a Deaf VI person has retinitis pigmentosa; he or she would have tunnel vision, depending on its severity and Visual Frame signing techniques will enable a signer to better match the receptive needs of the Deaf VI person. Visual Frame is, for the most part the same as BSL, but there are a number of adaptations required. For instance, finger-spelling, placement, role-shift, classifiers, facial expressions, lip patterns, referencing, eye gaze and back channeling should all be modified. These modifications differ, but for example finger-spelling can be adapted by the signer twisting their base hand outwards towards the Deaf VI person, which makes the shapes more visible to the receiver.

Other restrictions can occur due to visual impairment and

eye contact is an essential element for Visual Frame to work, especially when signs are typically articulated outside the user's field of vision: 'like', 'want', 'kidney', 'don't care'. Accordingly, a signal needs to be given that is within the Deaf VI person's field of vision and may be best achieved by a signer using their eyes to guide the receiver's eyes to move to the space that is outside their field of vision and then the sign can be produced.

Another particularly challenging restriction experienced by the majority of people with a visual impairment is their restricted perception of three-dimensional objects. With the inability to perceive depth, things such as steps and pot-holes just appear 'flat'—which is why the edge of stairs and steps in public places are a contrasting colour, as it helps people with a VI to differentiate between step and edge.

This restricted perception also poses specific problems for sign language users. For example the sign 'future' in un-adapted BSL has an open palm with closed fingers pointing forward, signifying that the future lies ahead. However if the receiver has a VI, their ability to perceive this sign is impaired, and their limited field of vision and depth of field perception may lead them to think the signer is waving at them. By adjusting the sign so that it is angled to the side (moving towards the left for right handed signers) the receiver is enabled to perceive the full meaning of the sign. Similarly, the sign 'yesterday', due to its position and movement, is commonly mistaken for the sign 'girl' or 'cry' by Deaf VI people. If the signer twists their head to the side, however, showing the side of the face that the sign is being performed on, the Deaf VI person can see the full sign.

These adaptations for a Visual Frame user are relatively simple. Visual Frame is only beneficial one-to-one, with effective use of eye contact and no visual distractions. Good lighting is required and the interpreter must wear clothing in a single colour with no patterns that contrasts with their skin tone. The majority of people with a visual impairment will be photophobic, i.e. have extreme sensitivity to light. Thus interpreters need to think about how and where they are positioned for an appropriate level of lighting. The light should be behind the person with the visual impairment and in front of the interpreter. This keeps the light out of the Deaf VI person's eyes and ensures the interpreter is illuminated.

When using Visual Frame, it is very important to ensure the Deaf VI person is included in the process. There are a number of things that interpreters can do to better improve the accessibility for sign language users with a restricted field of vision. In a conference setting, where two interpreters may be co-working, something as simple as clearly indicating the interpreter change-over can enable a Deaf VI person to shift their eye-gaze to the 'on' interpreter. Without this direct notification the Deaf VI person can often assume that the speaker has ceased their presentation, as it appears that the interpreter they were watching has just stopped signing. Small, thoughtful changes to practice can thus greatly benefit the Deaf VI user.

Hands-On

Hands-On is the adapted method for a person with little or no vision, i.e. when Visual Frame becomes impossible or impractical. Although BSL is a visual language, with no tactile components, Deaf people with a severe visual impairment, particularly Deaf people who have lost their sight, can only receive sign through the sense of touch. Consequently the first rule of signing to a Hands-On user is 'everything must always be tactile.' The Deaf VI person's hands are placed on top of the signer's hands, and the signer can move their hands freely, enabling the Hands-On user to 'feel' the language. The BSL features that in my experience require some adaptation are: specific hand shapes, finger-spelling, placement, role shift, referencing, classifiers and most importantly non-manual features (NMF).

As indicated by the name, NMF do not occur on the hands and are only visual in non-tactile BSL, it is therefore particularly important to adapt these when using Hands-On communication. NMF has many functions in BSL such as showing emotion, lexical distinction and grammar (Woll and Sutton-Spence, 1999: 96) and includes head nods/shakes, eyebrow raises and furrows, blinks, mouth gestures and mouthings. If BSL is not adapted the Deaf VI person is unable to access these nuances of the language. Hands-On has to incorporate all the features that would be typically transmitted though NMF, into the hands, at the same time as producing the signs.

In Hands-On communication, if the sign for 'work' is produced with very tight tension in the hand muscles, and moved very slowly, it allows the receiver to 'feel' what would normally be evident on the signer's face, conveying something like 'it's been a hard day at work'. However, if the same sign was produced with light tension in the signer's hand and performed slowly, the meaning would be that there was 'not much going on at work.' Thus the receiver can distinguish the meaning of this sign by feeling, as opposed to seeing the speed of the sign, how many times the sign is repeated, and how the signer utilises their signing space.

The concept of 'hand tension' is difficult to fully convey in a written format. Sign language interpreters are used to thinking visually rather than in a tactile way. However, tactile is the realm of the Hands-On user, and so when we sign in Hands-On we need to think in feelings; what can the person who is holding my hands 'feel' as opposed to what a Deaf person without a visual impairment can 'see'. This means that by changing the degree of tension in your hands, i.e. from very tight/tense to very loose and floppy, the Hands-On user will be able to 'feel' what you mean.

Ensuring that the Deaf VI person is fully included can be difficult in Hands-On. Although there are a number of different ways the interpreter to can position themselves within an interpreting environment, the interpreter always sits opposite the Deaf client. This means that objects like tables, heavy chairs, auditorium style halls, or even other people can present problems. I have experienced situations where the only chairs available for participants are fixed to the floor. On one occasion, my co-worker and I were provided with big lavish, armless chairs, which, whilst appropriate in the setting, were uncomfortable, heavy and made it difficult for us to move into a position which best suited the Deaf VI person.

Changing the system

In the UK there are two routes to qualify as a BSL/English interpreter, the postgraduate diploma and the NVQ route. Both have suitable opportunities for the insertion of specific training about working with Deaf VI people. In particular, the new level 3 NVQ certificate has to include twelve days of language development, which might be the perfect opportunity to teach the language adaptations for Hands-On and Visual Frame signing. Another would be to offer a workshop or short sessions spread over the duration of the interpreting course. Ideally, candidates would have the time and opportunity to practice in real-life situations. No matter how the course is structured, I strongly believe that interpreting with Deaf VI people should be a mandatory element in interpreting courses. Sweden, Switzerland, Finland, Canada and America include these features in their interpreter training. The UK should do likewise.

It is, however, important to stress that Visual Frame and Hands-On are not Deafblind communication methods, they are the communication methods used by Deaf people with a visual impairment. As a Deaf friend has commented, 'I'm Deaf first, my vision-loss is secondary—to say I'm not a BSL-user just because I have a visual impairment is awful.'

I am aware that this form of communication is not BSL in the conventional sense, but as interpreters we have a responsibility to the entire Deaf community. Whether or not they have any additional communication needs, we need to be prepared to meet these needs to the best of our ability; if we do not prepare trained and trainee interpreters for the variety of sign language users in the signing community we are neglecting our responsibility to that community.

Conclusion

I hope that this brief exploration of the culture and language of Deaf VI people and their methods of communication will highlight what interpreters need to do to accommodate these members of the Deaf community. I also hope that you now have a desire to make changes in our profession, so that we can provide access for the entire Deaf sign language using community, regardless of how they receive the language—be that tactile or visual, I do not think it should matter.

With appropriate training and practice, all the adaptations I have mentioned can become as natural to you as using conventional BSL. As long as we understand the culture and needs of Deaf VI people we can provide them with an interpreting service. If we do not make an effort to raise our awareness and do not undertake appropriate training, we neglect a large part of the sign language community.

References

British society of mental health and Deafness 2010: July http://www.bsmhd.org.uk/news0710.htm [accessed September 2010]

Kramsch, Claire. *Language and culture.* Oxford: OUP, 1998.

Sutton-Spence, Rachel and Bencie Woll. *The Linguistics of British Sign Language.* Cambridge: CUP, 1998.

Clearing the Pathways to Success— Supporting and Developing New Interpreters

Paul Belmonte and Jacqui Lees, Deaf Action

Starting work as an interpreter can be immensely challenging. For the new interpreter, every day brings unfamiliar situations, different people and the need to utilise skills which have only recently been acquired.

Many interpreters starting out on their career have a clear vision of where they would like to be and what they would like to achieve. For most, those objectives seem very distant and they may feel like they have a mountain to climb to realise them. It is a difficult fact of life that this 'mountain' has no cable car; the only way to the top is through time and through hard work. There are times when the pathways to becoming a confident and competent professional can seem to be strewn with obstacles.

However, many of the obstacles that get in the way of success can be minimised or overcome. Happily, the right kind of support can make the road to success much easier to navigate. Managers, colleagues and service users can have a profound effect on the early experiences of the novice interpreter and armed with the right tools, trainees or apprentices can find their early experiences to be challenging or exhilarating rather than unduly stressful.

Four of the main obstacles that can get in the way of success for a new interpreter were identified as:

- stress / fear
- lack of vision
- over-confidence
- lack of support.

Our workshop sought to define those obstacles and discuss ways of overcoming them.

Stress—what is it?

Feelings of stress are the body's response to what it perceives to be a dangerous or threatening situation. Physiological responses such as increased heart rate and the flow of adrenaline are designed to prepare us for 'fight or flight' situations. These responses can be helpful to us in challenging situations as they can keep us sharp and heighten ability in the short term.

Problems arise, however, when feelings of stress continue over a longer period or where there is 'a mismatch between our perceived demands and our perceived ability to cope.' (Looker & Gregson, 1997, p. 25) When the body is exposed to levels of stress beyond its ability to cope over a prolonged period of time, it can cause a wide range of health difficulties. Symptoms include high blood pressure, headaches, backache, tight neck and shoulders, frequent colds, fatigue or jaw pain. It can also lead to forgetfulness, problems with concentration, indecisiveness, irritability, anger, depression or panic attacks. It has been estimated that 'at least three quarters of those who visit their doctor have a stress-related complaint.' (*Ibid* p. 3)

Stress can have additional implications for sign language interpreters. Because we use our hands, arms, shoulders and bodies to such a great extent in our work, we have additional risks of upper limb disorders and repetitive strain injuries.

It is evident that everyone involved in the interpreting process has an interest in managing work-related stress.

What causes stress in new interpreters?

We contacted a number of apprentice and trainee interpreters to ask them the main causes of stress in their work. Some replied to a written questionnaire and others were interviewed by telephone or in person. The main things that cause stress were arranged into themes and the top three causes of anxiety were found to be as follows (along with some quotes from respondents):

1. Feeling inadequate

> ➢ 'looking incompetent'

> ➢ 'having to have things repeated and still not getting it'

> ➢ 'what if I can't cope?'

> ➢ 'feeling out of my depth'

Of course, all interpreters feel inadequate at times, but it is worth remembering that for new interpreters, this can be an everyday feeling!

2. Doing things for the first time

> ➤ 'Meeting the Deaf person for the first time . . . will I understand them? . . . will they LIKE me?'
>
> ➤ 'finding a new location'
>
> ➤ The first time in a certain type of assignment, e.g. a wedding.

It is easy to imagine (or remember!) the anxiety of receiving a certain assignment for the first time. For example, we may have been asked to interpret for Carolina in the Cardiology department of the hospital. We've never met Carolina and are not sure how she signs. We've never before been to that hospital; which bus goes there? Should we drive? Will we be able to park? We think cardiology has something to do with the heart, but have no idea what to expect from the appointment.

The same appointment one year later feels very different. We're looking forward to seeing Carolina again, we can't wait to hear about her holiday and wonder if her new medication is working well for her. It's a nice day, so we decide to take the bus. The relief of stress in these situations can often only come with experience and the passage of time.

3. The people we work with

> ➤ Coping with people being unaware of how to use an interpreter
>
> ➤ 'Deaf people telling us we're rubbish'
>
> ➤ 'my boss is demanding'
>
> ➤ 'will my co-worker be judging me? I wonder if they remember what it's like to be a trainee.'

It takes time to develop the coping strategies to deal with difficult people. It is particularly disappointing when the people who cause anxiety are the very ones who we might hope would be supportive of a less experienced interpreter.

How to cope
Stress is the body's way of dealing with a perceived threat, so dealing with the threat can be a first step in controlling the stress. It can be helpful to take a realistic look at the situation, see what is causing the stress and think about how it can be reduced.

It is important to develop new habits that distract or remove oneself from whatever is causing anxiety; this can help to manage stress on a more permanent basis. Useful habits can include:

- *Humour.* This produces helpful chemicals which aid relaxation and can also distract from stressful thoughts.

- *Exercise.* Even a quick walk in the fresh air can make a difference. Leave the building! Gentle stretching to warm up the body and limbs before an assignment can also relieve tension.

- *Keep hydrated.* Adequate amounts to drink through the day can stop us from feeling tired and lethargic but also lead to more visits to the toilet, which gives extra exercise and an excuse to leave stressful situations for a time.

The trainee interpreters who responded to our questions also shared some of the ways in which they cope:

- 'Learn and move on'
- Don't be afraid to slow things down

- Know your limitations
- Deep breathing / yoga
- Treats!

Other coping strategies can be summarised in three words: Plan, Expect and Communicate.

Plan

Careful planning of the diary and an awareness of the location of assignments can go a long way to alleviating stress.

The example was given of an interpreter (or their agency) being asked to attend an assignment at 12.30pm in a factory. They are already booked until 12.00 at the hospital across town, which is a twenty-five minute drive away, so the booking is accepted. The interpreter spends the whole morning looking at her watch and hoping the hospital appointment finishes on time. It does, but the interpreter is still feeling stressed and has to leave in a hurry, which upsets the Deaf client. Our interpreter hasn't had time to eat any lunch and gets more and more tense as she drives across town. Although she arrives at the factory on time, there is nowhere to park her car. So she rushes into her afternoon appointment 10 minutes late, which upsets the clients there, and of course her feelings of anxiety and the tension in her arms and shoulders means she does a poor piece of work. She leaves the factory with two more unhappy clients and feeling deskilled and demotivated. After a day like that, she wakes up the next morning with a cold and because of the previous day's events, does not feel motivated to go to work that day. Her appointments have to be cancelled, leaving yet more unhappy clients and the agency with a whole day's lost income. The interpreter (or their agency) was able to squeeze in an extra appointment on that day, but was it worth it?

This was a hypothetical situation, but everyone in the workshop recognised most of the elements as having been based on real life. If whoever accepts bookings plans properly and factors in things like lunch time and travel, it is not too difficult to avoid a large amount of the stress we face. How much better if the factory had been told that an interpreter could be provided, but not until 1.30!

Expect
Managing our own expectations and those of others can also help us to cope with feelings of stress. As a newer interpreter, we have to accept that some assignments will just not go well. That is normal. We can also take some reasonably simple steps to manage the expectations of others. Some of our respondents spoke of how difficult it can be to pluck up the courage to ask for a break in a longer assignment. A few minutes can be taken before the interpreting starts, to explain that there will be a break after twenty or thirty minutes, or maybe in some situations, that the interpreter may switch from simultaneous into consecutive interpreting. If everyone involved is prepared for what may happen, it can be much easier to cope with when these situations arise.

Communicate
Communication is possibly one of the most effective and important way of alleviating anxiety. New interpreters can make time to communicate with their manager, a mentor or possibly a counsellor. Those who are employed by an agency

or other body will hopefully have regular supervision sessions with a line manager.

However, even those who work as freelancers should make the time to talk to a trusted fellow professional. Time booked into the interpreting diary on a regular basis is invaluable and should not be neglected. 'Regular meeting . . . provides a good way for interpreters to build up their self esteem, which ultimately is the best defense against the negative effects of enduring stressful situations.' (Stewart, Schein & Cartwright 2004 p. 65)

Lack of vision and overconfidence

These obstacles are less common among newer interpreters, but they can occur from time to time so it is worth giving them brief consideration. When we get into the routine of our work as an interpreter, it becomes easier to look no further ahead than the next assignment. As we live and work from day to day, we can sometimes become fixated on the path that is immediately ahead of us and forget the summits to which we aspire.

It is helpful for all of us to have clear aims in mind and a well-planned strategy for achieving them. Goals we may have set are only of any use if we remember them and take steps to achieve them. It is helpful to record the objectives we have set for ourselves and to regularly take stock of our progress.

Overconfidence is another obstacle which can get in the way of success. An interpreter who suffers from a surfeit of confidence is blind to the areas in which they need to improve and therefore will struggle to achieve success as a professional. They may also accept assignments for which they are not sufficiently experienced and do actual damage in those situations.

Fellow professionals have some responsibility here; for the good of the communities in which we work and of the interpreter themselves, we may need to help our newer colleagues to have a more realistic view of their abilities and the fields in which they should be working.

However, it was mentioned in the workshop that over-confidence in a new interpreter is actually quite rare. Some might put on a brave face and project an air of confidence when in fact they are very unsure of themselves and their abilities. For a colleague to 'bring them down a peg or two' could actually do untold damage to their already fragile confidence.

So, when attempting to help someone who we may perceive to be overconfident, there is a need to approach the situation with tact and sensitivity. We do need to make sure that our clients receive the best service possible and it is vital that we do all we can to protect the reputation of our profession. However, we need to take care not to cause harm to our colleagues who may be well aware of their faults and who may be damaged by overly harsh criticism.

On the other hand, new interpreters should try to have a realistic view of their current abilities. It is helpful when they can be honest with their colleagues if fear and trepidation might tempt them to project a front which might me misconstrued as overconfidence.

How others can help

A fourth obstacle that can get in the way of success for new interpreters can be a lack of support. Conversely, we should never underestimate the difference the rest of us can make in supporting interpreters with less experience. As colleagues, managers or those involved with interpreter associations, we can have a huge impact on the feelings and confidence of the people we work with.

Training providers
Coping skills can be imparted at the earliest stages of an interpreter's career, even while they are undergoing their initial training programme. Successful training providers have recognised the need to teach such skills as reflective practice, both as an individual and with supportive peers. Work placements can help students to understand the demands of working in the real world as well as building valuable relationships for the future. Furthermore, students benefit greatly from positive encouragement and feedback which builds confidence and helps them develop as individuals and as professionals. (Sarah Bown, School of Law, Social Sciences and Communications, University of Wolverhampton—email communication to the authors, 6 September 2010)

Interpreter Associations
We contacted a number of interpreter associations and asked them what they have in place to support newer members. Our aim was not to find gaps in provision or to criticise any organisation, but to find and highlight good practice wherever it occurs.

One strategy used in a number of countries was the provision of mentors. The mentor will work with the trainee on an individual basis, looking at their work and helping to improve their skills. These discussions can also provide vital support as confidence issues are explored. As a representative of one interpreter association told us, 'We hope that they share their enthusiasm with each other and lend a hand when needed.' It was also noted that 'the mentor gets as much from the relationship as the mentee.'

In another country, students have the opportunity to spend time with working interpreters. As well as sharing skills and experience, students form professional relationships at an early stage, which will be of support to them as they progress in their career.

One association provides a telephone counselling service, whereby all members, including trainees, can call in complete confidence to discuss any kind of issues, whether work related or personal.

Another country provides an on-line buddy programme, where members with varying experience can discuss ethics, professional conduct, semantics and other issues.

Agencies

Agencies who employ interpreters play a key role in their development. The pathway to success can begin right from day one, at the induction stage. As well as basic and mandatory training, a successful induction package will include evaluation and feedback. A new member of staff can also benefit from what is called a FOFO induction, meaning 'Find Out For Oneself'. Doing research, meeting people from related organisations and getting involved in various tasks and projects can help the employee to take responsibility for their own learning and quickly feel a part of the organization and the community.

It is helpful when someone joining the communication support team is encouraged to meet Deaf people at every opportunity. These relaxed, informal conversations can do a great deal to build the language skills and confidence of someone new to the profession. Deaf clients also enjoy the opportunity to meet new staff and build a rapport with them. It also helps to build confidence when new interpreters are able to spend time (possibly the first month or so) shadowing other members of the team, watching them work and being given the opportunity to do a small amount of work when appropriate with the support of their colleagues.

We contacted a number of interpreter agencies and asked what they do to support new staff. Some provide each new member of staff with an allocated buddy, someone who is a good match to that individual's personality and experience. Having someone assigned as a personal buddy helps the trainee to appreciate they are not being a nuisance in asking for support. In other places, peer discussion groups are set up to talk about dilemmas, share experiences and offer assistance.

Irrespective of whoever supports a trainee interpreter in the workplace, it can be useful to discuss the setting of specific goals and to give honest and positive feedback on how those goals have been achieved. Training sessions are also valuable. As well as increasing an interpreter's knowledge and skills, they also contribute to a feeling of being encouraged and valued. One agency even mentioned that they had provided training in stress management, which is sure to be helpful!

Some agencies mentioned the need to carefully monitor the amount of time spent interpreting. Some set a maximum number of interpreting hours of between twenty and twenty-five hours per week. (As recommended in Frishberg, 1990, p. 78) This helps to combat fatigue, but also allows staff to have at least some time in the office each week to prepare for assignments, reflect on work carried out and share support time with colleagues.

It is equally important to take care with the types of jobs allocated to trainees. As one agency manager told us, 'Confidence can be fragile, so trainees are not forced to take on jobs they're not ready for.' Newer interpreters can also have the opportunity to observe more complex assignments before being asked to carry them out themselves.

Mentoring and supervision

One of the most important ways of supporting new interpreters is through regular, one to one discussions with a line manager or mentor. An agency manager may view it as good practice to hold regular supervision sessions with staff. They may also make an effort to be available between supervisions to talk through any difficult situations which may have arisen. Discussions can take place after an assignment between a trainee interpreter and a more experienced co-worker. These sessions can do much to help a trainee to quickly move towards confidence, competence and happiness at work.

It should be said though, that at times these discussions may not be as helpful as they could be. To illustrate this, the participants in the workshop were asked to work in pairs. One person from each pair was asked to act the part of a trainee interpreter who had just completed a difficult job with a more experienced team interpreter. The trainee was asked to express their feelings at having done a poor piece of work. The other person in the pair was given one printed response from a possible three. Some were told to mention a list of things the trainee had done badly in the assignment. Others were told to list a number of things which had made the assignment difficult. They were told to be careful to say nothing positive to the discouraged trainee. The third possible response was to deny that anything at all had gone wrong and tell the trainee that their work had been entirely wonderful.

It was clear from the atmosphere in the room that these discussions were not going well, so as a group, we discussed how everyone felt. We noted down some of their feedback:

- ➢ Negative comments make you feel like you want to give up
- ➢ Confuses—feedback not that helpful
- ➢ It is nice to get positive feedback but when you know it is not completely truthful then you lose faith in it
- ➢ Solid feedback is needed to help in that situation
- ➢ Know that you are a trainee, know your limitations as a trainee and use your co-worker in the best way
- ➢ Positive feedback is good and when the qualified interpreter tells of their own experiences then it is very helpful
- ➢ When you are in a similar situation again, review from the last time and see if things have changed
- ➢ Co-worker has to take responsibility as well if a job goes badly

The participants then worked as pairs one more time to try to make the experience more positive and helpful. It was agreed that these sessions should be balanced; honest about what hadn't worked well but at the same time positive about the trainee's skills and with clear goals set to aid improvement.

Success is possible

When starting out in our profession, we soon realise that we have a mountain to climb. Progress is only possible through time and hard work. However, many of the obstacles that get in the way can be minimised or overcome.

We closed the workshop with a number of quotes from trainee interpreters who are evidently coping well with the stresses and anxieties that can come with entering our profession:

- 'I am supported by a fantastic team'
- 'I know the assignment will be over in an hour. . . I've been in labour for eighteen hours, so I know I can do this!'
- 'I have the most supportive employers I've ever had in my life . . . My workplace is friendly, supportive, comfortable and safe.'

Whether we are a new interpreter, a more experienced practitioner, a manager, someone involved in an interpreter association or a service user, we all share a common aim: for new interpreters to quickly become confident, competent and happy. All of us have an important role to play in making sure this happens and all of us benefit when it does.

References

Andrews, Linda Wasmer (2005) *Stress Control for Peace of Mind,* London: Greenwich Editions

Frishberg, Nancy (1990) *Interpreting—An Introduction (revised edition),* Silver Spring MD: RID Publications

Harrington, Frank J. and Turner, Graham H. (2001) *Interpreting Interpreting* , Coleford, UK: Douglas McLean

Looker, Terry and Gregson, Olga (1997) *Teach Yourself – Managing Stress,* London: Hodder Education

Stewart, David A., Schein, Jerome D. and Cartwright, Brenda E. (2004) *Sign Language Interpreting – Exploring Its Art and Science* Boston: Allyn and Bacon

Wadensjö, Cecilia (1998) *Interpreting As Interaction,* New York: Addison Wesley Longman

Keep the balance—
Holistic Stress Prevention

Ralf Weibel

Is our job as stressful as any other common job? Do we lack in self care because we ignore our personal needs? What are the benefits of living a balanced professional life?

Our work involves sitting in-between two parties who argue with each other, confront us with contradictory emotions, or just confuse the inner balance we had before interpreting the assignment. These are common phenomena for a sign language interpreter. They result in the assumption that these experiences are business as usual and part of our daily work life. To earn money, being busy and having crowded schedules is customary, tolerated and accepted in our profession. Thus, time becomes a rare commodity.

Why should we take care for ourselves? A healthy body and mind is necessary to function successfully in our professional field. Nurturing personal needs starts with paying attention to the personal situation. Consequently, it means investing in body and mind—our personal well-being—the essential of being able to function and bear the demands of work life is health. To achieve a healthy and robust constitution it is indispensable to find time for nurturing the body, mind and soul.

But how do we gain time in an age where time seems to

be limited and the most valuable good? Some people live in timelessness without any free capacitiy, others are able to find a free minute for whatever they intend to do or that arises. Surprisingly, all these people have the same amount of time—twenty-four hours a day, from now until the end of his/her life.

But what distinguishes the former from the latter: a couple of hours stolen from the continuum of time, used to annoy others by showing them that having time is not impossible? If you want to care for yourself, time seems to be the important issue. No single minute left in your schedule? 'I have no time for it' means nothing more than 'This is not important to me.' If something matters to you, a certain amount of time will be found for sure. If prevention measurements and your own health are important to you, time can be found in a day with twenty-four hours. The first step towards it is spending time *for* and *with* yourself on a regular basis to recuperate. These timeouts are also essential to gain anoverview of your general situation as well.

Showing symptoms of distress however does not necessarily mean that your professional life is imbalanced. It just reveals that you are not in balance and your challenge is to find out where the stress comes from. Take time to ask yourself what your priorities are. Your favourite activities are the parts of the day that seem to be more important to you as opposed to other activities where 'no time' is your argument. Does self care belong to one of the 'no time' arguments or are you willing to arrange your schedule and start to care? Do not forget that your spare time is the only time you can actively prevent imbalances. Your efforts will not be in vain.

The advantages of taking time for practising self care are manifold. First of all, your physical constitution improves. The body becomes more able to cope with a heavy workload and becomes more robust. You will be fitter and feel healthier. As a consequence, work performance improves due to a better constitution, a relaxed attitude and the ability to be focused on the spot for a longer period of time. Thus, it is not just your body, mind and soul that profits but also your clients and colleagues. The reason is simply your improved ability to cope with strain and the demands of the assignments results in an improved performance.

Nevertheless, our professional lives are likely to remain demanding. The efforts of concentration, making instantaneous decisions and being flexible require a lot of energy. Experiencing exactly this in our everyday life creates a subcultural stereotype of what the life of a sign language interpreter has to be like. Automatically, an inner expectation of occupational risks and illness typical for the profession is formed. We start to assume we have no time, only strains and burdens. Instead of listening to these potential subconscious expectations, listen to your personal needs. Try to have space for the unexpected, take care for yourself and find a balance between workload and personal needs. Take the time to find your own way of preventing ill health.

Finding time to actively prevent and nurture your body and mind tells you something about how important preservation is for and to yourself. Your body, along with your spirit, will need this care. The presenter's balanced way of putting holistic stress prevention into practise is to love the profession, and live the profession, but not exclusively live for the profession.

'Well, it's green here, but I've seen green and green, and my mother's was always green': initial issues and insights from translating the BSL Corpus.

Kyra Pollitt, Janet Beck, Helen Dunipace, Sue Lee, Cathryn McShane, Elvire Roberts, Sherratt Rowan & Robert Skinner, and Adam Schembri & Graham H. Turner.

The title of this paper is a genuine translation of a signed utterance taken from data gathered for the British Sign Language (BSL) Corpus Project. It was an older deaf woman's response to a question posed on the subject of variation in BSL signs for colours.

Of course, when you first read that translated sentence you had little or no context to help you create sense and determine meaning, but the translation you see before you not only appears odd in British English (a language which tends not to show variation of colour terms), it also masks the richness of the original.

It's the perfect place to begin our discussion of some of the issues faced and insights gained by the team of translators engaged in translating sections of the BSL Corpus Project (BSLCP) data. When this paper was originally presented, at the ASLI conference of 2010, the translation work was still ongoing. Although the first phase of the BSL Corpus Project is now complete, this paper reflects the initial thoughts of a translation team still grappling with the practices and practicalities of this work. Thus, although at the time of publication this first phase of translation has been completed, this paper reproduces the concerns and thoughts of a team still engaged in the activity.

The BSL Corpus Project

The BSL Corpus Project was funded by the Economic and Social Research Council and led by Dr. Adam Schembri of the DCAL (Deafness, Cognition and Language) Research Centre at the University College London (UCL) in collaboration with the University of Bangor, Bristol University, Queen's University in Belfast and Heriot-Watt (Edinburgh), where Professor Graham H. Turner, Director of The Centre for Translation and Interpreting Studies in Scotland (CTISS) and himself a BSL specialist, held primary responsibility for the translation element of the BSLCP.

The project ran from January 2008 to December 2010, and aimed to create an on-line, open-access collection of BSL digital video data to facilitate research on variation and change in the language.

To this end a number of deaf fieldworkers were recruited: Avril Hepner, Carolyn Nabarro, Dawn Marshall, Evelyn McFarland, Jacqueline Parker, Jeff Brattan-Wilson, Jenny Wilkins, Mark Nelson, Melinda Napier, Mischa Cooke and Sarah Lawrence. The fieldworkers were charged with filming approximately thirty deaf native and near-native signers (defined as having had BSL exposure by seven years of age) in eight regions across the UK (sites of current or former residential deaf schools with sufficiently large deaf communities to make the balanced recruitment of participants according to age, gender, ethnicity etc. possible): London, Bristol, Birmingham, Manchester, Newcastle, Cardiff, Glasgow and Belfast.

This yielded a total sample of 249 individuals (ranging from those in their teens to those in their eighties, most having lived in their region for ten years or more), each of whom told a two to ten minute personal experience story, engaged in thirty minutes of free conversation, was interviewed for twenty minutes and undertook a ten minute vocabulary task.

The Brief

This is the first of the large-scale sign language corpora (compare sign language corpus projects in Australia, the Netherlands, Germany etc.) to include written English translation as part of its publicly accessible platform, so there is no direct precedent to work to, nor from which to deviate.

In addition, the data will be made available via the internet, so the question of audience design for the translation (Munday, 2001) becomes somewhat thorny. Who is likely to want to access the BSL data through the translation, and why? The potential audience ranges from BSL natives and users of other sign languages seeking to improve their English or BSL skills, through linguists unfamiliar with this (or, perhaps any other) sign language using the translation to help them locate and understand points of academic interest, to those concerned with the study of acts of translation *per se*, and beyond to future users with purposes we may not yet conceive. How might one 'write to this audience'?

Then there's the content. Let us take you back to the title of this piece. The data was primarily collected for the purpose of documenting and analysing variation and change in BSL across a number of geographically widespread sites. The language samples collected are, not surprisingly, rich in homonyms, steeped in local habit and culture and populated by local characters.

A 'free translation' (Vinay and Darbelnet, 1958/1995) might begin to offer a taste of the strong flavour of these pieces through the introduction of regional variants from spoken English (e.g. '*dunsh*' for crash/bump in Newcastle 'Geordie' English). There are, however, a number of problems with this approach: (i) these non-standard English variants often have contested orthographic forms, so spelling would be a matter of intuition and guesswork, (ii) the variations in English terms are unlikely to appear at the same junctures as the variations in BSL (e.g. colour terms), so would effectively demonstrate variation in British English rather than allowing the reader to access variation in BSL, and (iii) the English text produced in this way would not be accessible to readers who do not have a high level of fluency in British English (e.g. native speakers of Australian or American English who are unfamiliar with British regionalisms, not to mention non-native English users in the wider international context).

At the other extreme a literal translation, although certainly 'foreignising' the text in some ways (Venuti 2000), would surely backfire given the sadly persistent misconception of sign languages as spoken/written languages 'on the hands', or worse, sub-languages. Elsewhere, a team of linguists and researchers have been tasked with 'ID glossing' the data (with ID glossing, each sign will have its own unique identifying English gloss, and sign variants will be distinguished by a number, consistently throughout all the annotation files—this will make it possible to search the corpus for specific sign forms, regardless of possibly varying English translations for the same sign).

In the end it was agreed that the two to ten minute personal experience stories (narratives) and the twenty minute interviews would be the focus of the translation activity, and that the translation brief was to produce 'clear, fluent, conversational, standard English', 'reflecting the informal, chatty style of the interviews and narratives' and 'the norms of casual conversation for the gender and age of the participant.'

Although this might seem a clear guiding principle, it is in fact riddled with uncertainty and difficulty. The first of these is the writing of conversational English. How should this look? For example, it is not always clear in conversation when a sentence has ended or begun. How should this be punctuated within 'fluent . . . standard English' (without reverting to the conventions of conversational analysis, say)?

Conversations tend not to use exclusively standard forms of English, but are riddled with common contractions such as 'dunno' for 'don't know', 'innit?' for 'isn't it?' and the increasingly widespread use of the discourse marker 'like'. Which of these forms might be accessible to our audience, and which impenetrable? What happens to the conversational affect if the more formal, non-contracted form is used in the translation?

Thus the number of caveats to our simple original directive increases as the work of translation progresses; for example, a codiçil has been added permitting the occasional inclusion of spoken English variants when both the source and target text are able to deviate simultaneously, and where the translator can insert a bracketed explanation of the English term.

Dealing with the ever-expanding number of codiçils would be difficult enough for one translator, but The Pollitt Bureau (which won the translation contract) has divided the translation task between eight translators, each of whom has some familiarity with the sign language community of a specific region from which BSLCP data was collected. These translators (named above) are each supported by a translation consultant, usually one of the original deaf fieldworkers. The translation consultants are Dawn Marshall, Carolyn Nabarro, Avril Hepner, Jeff Brattan-Wilson, Melinda Napier, Rosemary Oram, Marie Franklin, and Tom Johnston. This team approach echoes the original data collection methodology and is designed to render the richest and most informed translations possible. However, it does also present a number of logistical challenges, not least of which is keeping the whole, geographically dispersed team of sixteen 'on message' with the evolving brief.

Any linguist will also tell you that in conversation a great deal of meaning is conveyed through intonation, gesture and facial expression; all of which has to be expressed rather differently in written English. When the source text is a conversation in a visual-gestural modality, capturing and codifying such information in written, linear form becomes that much more challenging.

The question of Cinderella's slipper

The BSLCP translators face all the usual issues of translation between signed and spoken/written languages, and some rather more interesting challenges besides. However, given the lack of literature exploring the growing field of translation between signed and orthographic language forms, it is worth rehearsing some of the core issues here.

Firstly, let's clarify our basic terms. We are looking here at translation, not interpretation. We are defining that as working from one recorded medium into another recorded medium, outwith real time constraints. Translation affords the opportunity to rewind or review the source text and to construct, reconstruct and review the target text during production (for explorations of norms of translation see Toury, 1978/1995). The target text is then fixed, and usually open to scrutiny.

The greatest challenges our translators face arise from what has been termed 'materiality of mode' (Kress, 2003, 45). This refers to the fabric (materiality) of the message. In our case, we are working between two very different modes with very different materialities. What written English looks like, and what it can and cannot do differs enormously from what is possible and what is constrained in recorded sign language. For example, sign language texts are not 'written' or read from left to right. Written English does not place tokens in (three dimensional) space and then refer back to them by highlighting spatial position. Written English texts find it difficult to construct sentences without placing tokens in the principal grammatical slots; sign language texts often do not (Nilsson, 2010).

This mismatch of materialities between the language pair in signed/written language translation seems likely to be one of the more extreme of any language pairing. This makes the work of the translator so much more difficult than that of a colleague working between more similar language pairs (with little difference in materiality of mode) such as written French and written Spanish.

With such disparity between materialities of mode, it is perhaps not surprising that the two language communities exhibit quite distinct cultural differences. These can have great bearing on the act of translation. Differences in discoursal practices such as story- or joke-telling evolve directly from this heady mix of materiality and culture. It falls to the translator to try to find resolution to the story that is entertainingly visual in BSL but long-winded, flat and purposeless in written English, or the joke that is pithy, punchy and intertextually rich in written English but hollow, brief and lacking visual play in BSL.

Adding to this already difficult task is the relationship between the two languages; the powerful, globally dominant position of English and its role in relation to the misunderstood, minority language of a 'disabled' people must be handled with some sensitivity. The capitalisation of the letter 'd', for example, is an ever more carefully considered political act. The translator must tread carefully and be very aware of their role and the potential effects of their acts of translation.

To mark or not to mark, is that the question?

It is only with the advent of technology that translation has become a practical alternative to interpreting practices between signed/written languages. Even so, the occasions on which sign languages were recorded onto Beta or VHS videotapes were circumscribed, for many years limited to domains such as television broadcasts.

The widespread availability of digital technology, and changes in patterns of signed text production and consumption stimulated by the internet have allowed translation to emerge as a new and growing field of practice. The number of interpreters at the conference presentation of this paper who acknowledged that their regular working practices involved translation of one form or another (including sight translation, see Pöchhacker, 2004, p.19) was significant.

The 'Cinderella's slipper' considerations sketched above are par for the course in signed/written language translation. Yet the BSLCP translators face a number of other, less usual challenges: the technology used in the project throws down a gauntlet, challenging us to upgrade and update our translation practices. Returning to our title sentence provides an illustration of this.

Whilst a fair translation of the original utterance, as we have already determined, our title sentence is unable to show or even to adequately hint at the variation of colour term available in the original. But what if the translation appears concurrently with the original signed text? Does this solve the translator's dilemma?

The BSL Corpus translations are being written directly into ELAN[1], a freely downloadable software programme developed by The Max Planck Institute for Psycholinguistics. The ELAN interface shows a video screen of the original signed source

---

1 http://www.lat-mpi.eu/tools/elan/

text. To the right of this are a number of controls, allowing the reader to search, slow down, speed up, replay etc. Below this a number of 'tiers' are available, each scrolling from right to left in text format. The number of tiers can be customised to purpose. In our case there are many tiers showing, for example on one tier ID glossing, on another hand shape configuration for the right hand et cetera. Since all the participants were filmed in pairs, there are two tiers carrying the translation; one for Participant One and another for Participant Two (this is particularly important where there is back channelling or overlapping 'talk'). The translation is added in 'time segments', synchronised with the sign language utterance (where there are differences in length between the sign language utterance and the written translation, providing the translator has selected the time segment according to the span of the source text, the translation will simply wrap around within that time segment). This means that whenever the reader activates the sign language video, the information on the tiers scrolls along in time to the source text.

In some ways, then, this should allow the translator some slack, alleviating the pressure to expand on utterances that are accompanied by visual clues. Where the signer says 'Over there' and points, the translator in ELAN should not have to add {points to right hand corner of screen}, as this can be seen by the viewer. Or should they?

Much of our team discussion thus far has been taken up with these kinds of negotiations around the technology. What if the reader is not familiar at all with signed languages and is unlikely to be able to identify the exact point in the signed utterance where this particular pointing action occurs?

What if this same reader is looking at colour term variation in this strange and confusing visual gestural language, and is navigating by the translation? Would our title sentence, with its 'green and green' prove sufficient compass? After a great deal of debate we decided that the presence of a regional variant that is specifically given as an example should be indicated by the insertion of some sort of symbol before the translated word, such as '[*] green'. This seemed a reasonable compromise that would at least alert the reader to something going on in the source text that is not apparent in the target text.

But then doesn't '[*] green and [*] green' still imply that the signs used are the same? We began to attribute numbers to each of the sign variants, taking care to ensure that each variant's number was used consistently. This led to sentences such as 'Well, it's [*1] green here, but I've seen [*3] green and [*4] green, and my mother's was always [*2] green'.

We then realised that if each translator in each region used the same coding system there was a danger that, to someone navigating the entire dataset via the translation, a variant of the sign GREEN used in Bristol might appear the same as a completely distinct variant of the sign GREEN used in Newcastle, since they might both be marked as [*1] green.

Each translator now has their own symbol, [*], [~], [^] et cetera, and is responsible for ensuring that the symbol and numbering of the variants are consistent throughout the translation of their regional data set. However, we were unable to cross-reference all the sign variants across regions. Thus if, by strange co-incidence, our title sentence were to appear in two regions it might be represented as 'Well, it's [*1] green here, but I've seen [*3] green and [*4] green, and my mother's was always [*2] green' in one region, and 'Well, it's [^2] green here, but I've seen [^4] green and [^1] green, and my mother's was always [^3] green' in another, regardless of whether the signs used were in fact the same in both regions or entirely different.

This is to some extent an exercise in future-proofing the translations, ensuring they might still be fit for purpose as navigational technology evolves.

It has, however, also muddied the waters between the

activities of the linguists working on the other tiers and the translators, since the linguists *will* be cross-referencing the sign variants across the whole of the corpus (ID glossing). Perhaps a lesson for future corpora is to ensure that the translators and linguists allow ample time for ongoing dialogue about translation and annotation issues, so that the translations and linguistic annotations are consistent with and complement each other as much as possible.

Technology and translation at the cutting edge
Whether or not we have made the right decisions in the translation of the BSLCP data, there is no doubt that the technology is 'actant' in the translation process (Brandt and Clinton, 2002: 338). That is, the technology shapes and dictates certain parameters and activities within the translation process. There is no doubt that these translations would be different were they to have been undertaken using pen and paper or even keyboard, for example, to be published in a booklet alongside a videotape.

The real-time presence of the visual source text presents interesting questions on the degree to which the form of the target text should be designed to complement the source text. The translator has to develop new skills in creating time segments that finely match the source text utterance, and so on. Each and all of these considerations break new ground in translation practices and offer opportunities to expand the field of translation studies (see Wurm, 2010 for a more in-depth discussion of related themes).

But it is not just in the act of translation that the BSL Corpus Project is breaking new ground. The translation team are using technology in innovative ways to manage and co-negotiate the translation activity.

It is most unusual to find a project that involves such a large team of translators, and consultants, working together.

The sixteen individuals involved all live in different locations, and it is technology that is providing the solution to managing the team. Of course email is very important, and web-based file sharing facilities are proving invaluable for the exchange and comparison of large source text video files. Perhaps the biggest boon, however, has been the creation of a private area on a social networking site where translators and consultants are sharing their thoughts, frustrations, questions and solutions as the work progresses. Indeed, the messages posted on this site by the translators have informed this presentation and paper. The social networking site postings not only allow for management and dissemination of information, sharing and co-negotiation of the task, they create a written record of the questions, frustrations and solutions involved in the translation process. This is data in its own right. In addition, each translator has been asked to keep a personal diary, and it is hoped these thoughts and insights will inform future papers and serve to further develop the growing field of signed/written language translation studies. Readers will have to consult future publications for reflections on this aspect of the first phase of BSLCP translation experience.

The trouble with time . . . and management . . . and expectation . . .

One of the other ways in which such a large project, with such a large team, can contribute to the field is in adding to our understanding of the quotidian practicalities of translation work. From the moment of deciding to add translation to the publicly accessible project platform, we had several questions. How long should a sample translation take? How much, therefore, should be set aside for the budget?

These simple questions are not easy to answer. Individual translators are likely to work at different speeds and at different speeds on different texts, and may employ different means of arriving at a translation. The complexity of source texts may vary linguistically (perhaps someone with a very obscure dialect of BSL, perhaps a number of participants engaging in witty repartee) or in terms of content (perhaps a story about the technical intricacies of motorcycle mechanics), or indeed in terms of technology (data accidentally filmed from a difficult camera angle, or with insufficient light). The translator's degree of familiarity with the technology of target text creation will also play a part.

Such factors will always remain variable, but there is no current industry standard or expectation against which to measure or to which to add a margin of error. By involving a number of individuals, working in similar circumstances, the BSL Corpus Project translation may begin to redress this lack.

The recruitment of translators began in May/June 2010 and all the translations must be completed by the end of December, 2010. The Project should produce, in total, 816 hours of translation (136 days) and 144 hours of consultancy (24 days). The hours spent with a consultant are included in the translator's hours. Each translator has 10 hours of data (one has 11), and 102 hours of translation time (17 days of work). This gives each translator roughly 10 hours of translation and consultancy time per hour of data. The actual number of translations completed within the hours and budget available, together with the reflections and comments of the translators, recorded as they engage with the task, should reveal some useful bench marks for future translation project planners.

References

Deborah Brandt and Katie Clinton, 'Limits of the Local: Expanding Perspectives on Literacy as a Social Practice'. *Journal of Literacy Research* 34.3 (2002) 337–355

Trevor Johnston and Adam Schembri 'Issues in the creation of a digital archive of a signed language' in *Sustainable data from digital fieldwork* eds. L. Barwick and N. Thieberger, (Sydney: University of Sydney Press, 2006) 7–16.

Gunther Kress, *Literacy in the New Media Age* (London and New York: Routledge, 2003), 45.

Anna-Lena Nilsson, 'Studies in Swedish Sign Language: Reference, Real Space Blending, and Interpretation' (PhD diss., University of Stockholm, 2010)

Jeremy Munday, *Introducing translation studies: theories and applications* (London and New York: Routledge, 2001).

Franz Pöchhacker, *Introducing Interpreting Studies* (London and New York: Routledge, 2004), 1.4.2

Gideon Toury, 'The nature and role of norms in translation' in *The Translation Studies Reader* ed. Lawrence Venuti (London and New York: Routledge, 2002) 198–213

Lawrence Venuti, 'Translation, community, utopia' in *The Translation Studies Reader* ed. Lawrence Venuti (London and New York: Routledge, 2002) 468–488

Jean-Paul Vinay and Jean Darbelnet 'A methodology for translation', trans: Juan C. Sager and M. J. Hamel, in *The Translation Studies Reader* ed. Lawrence Venuti (London and New York: Routledge, 2002) 88–92

Svenja Wurm 'Translation across modalities: the practice of translating written text into recorded sign language—an ethnographic case study' (PhD diss., Heriot-Watt University, 2010)

> Contact details:
> www.bslcorpusproject.org
> kyra@thepollittbureau.com

'Safe to Practice'—A holistic approach to interpreter assessment

Maureen Saville & Stuart Anderson

Introduction

In line with the 2010 ASLI conference theme 'Developing the interpreter; developing the profession' this paper aims to share knowledge and generate new reflections on the selection, development and assessment of sign language interpreters, based on one assessment centre's experience. It will look at the development of best practice and the approach to course structures, assessment processes and techniques for support that can be offered to students and candidates undertaking interpreting programmes.

Background

Any training and assessment provider should place a high emphasis not only on providing routes to certification but also on the establishment of foundations that enable life-long reflective practice and the skill development of individuals on those programmes. This paper aims to give an insight into the journey that interpreters who train with the assessment centre Signamic Ltd take - from entry level skills development through to becoming qualified interpreters and beyond. It will cover the interview and selection process for admission, the development programmes offered, how trainee interpreters are developed through training combined with practicum in safe controlled environments, and will explain processes used to determine when candidates are ready to move onto the final assessment stage of a programme. This paper will also discuss adjustments that can be made to meet individual needs during the assessment process, and how to continue to support students once they have achieved MRSLI[1] status.

Ensuring high and consistent levels of quality should be the philosophy of any training provider, and this paper will elaborate on how we work with organisations such as Signature to ensure the highest possible standards in training provision and interpreter output.

Interview—what we look for at application stage and how we do this

The Signature Level 6 NVQ Diploma in Sign Language Interpreting qualification consists of two parts: the skills and knowledge development part: Level 6 NVQ Diploma in Sign Language Interpreting: Part 1 (INT6/1), and the skills assessment part: Level 6 NVQ Diploma in Sign Language Interpreting: Part 2 (INT6/2).

Therefore students admitted to Level 6 NVQ Diploma in Sign Language Interpreting: Part 1 will go through a taught programme, which will typically take around 16 full days over eight months (or 96 class contact hours). This development phase offers students the opportunity to acquire the knowledge, skills, academic and practical tools they will need in order to undertake the next and final stage, which is the Signature Level 6 NVQ Diploma in Sign Language Interpreting:

---

1 Member of the Register of BSL/English Interpreters

Part 2.

Interview Process: A Holistic Approach to Assessment

Interview for admission to the development course (Level 6 NVQ Diploma in Sign Language Interpreting: Part 1) takes one full day. We are looking for a high level of skills in BSL (the expectation is that applicants will have achieved, or can demonstrate BSL skills equivalent to, Signature NVQ Level 6), English skills equivalent to Level 7 on the CILT Languages Ladder and interpreting skills and experience (CILT 2011).

In addition to these areas of competence, individuals need to demonstrate that they are able to present the world with well-rounded interpreter who is suitably equipped to manage the demands of working in varied domains with a range of consumer expectations. It is for this reason that during the interview/selection day, a candidate's attitude, self-evaluation skills and ability to work under pressure are also assessed. The structure and aims of our selection process have been influenced by the work of Karen Bontempo and her research into the notion of interpreter aptitude in relation to interpreter personality. In her presentation to the 2009 Supporting Deaf People Online conference she commented:

> 'It would appear that successful performance as an interpreter is dependent on dimensions of cognitive ability (for example, general intelligence, memory capacity, processing speed, attention span etc) AND personality factors (such as anxiety, motivation, stress-resistance, emotional sensitivity, and confidence, among others).' (Bontempo 2009)

In addition to this, at the Aptitude for Interpreting symposium in Antwerp in May 2009, she concluded her presentation with the comments that data collected thus far indicates that interviewers who wish to select for success, select individuals who are conscientious and emotionally adjusted. She further recommends that development programmes include assertiveness and resilience skills in the curricula, and that interpreting students are taught how to better manage anxiety.

It is with this in mind that the interviews are structured so that the applicants are assessed both as a group and as individuals, and are presented with tasks that will require them to utilise pragmatic coping strategies and manage themselves in relation to the demands placed upon them during the interview process. This enables the assessors to observe how the candidates react on an emotional level to those demands, and how they interact with other candidates undergoing the same process.

Interview Structure INT6/1

To develop familiarity with the NVQ assessment, the interview for admission to the INT6/1 development course is structured in line with the units from the INT6/2 NVQ programme. This enables interviewers to gain an insight into the candidates' level of skill, experience and knowledge in each specific area, and at the same time supports the formulation of an Individual Interpreter Development Plan (IIDP) (which also follows the NVQ unit structure).

The assessment tasks are as follows: English comprehension, one-way interpreting, two-way interpreting (incorporating a co-interpreted exercise), written preparation and self-evaluation for both interpreting tasks, a questionnaire and one-to-one interview. The assessors stay with the group throughout the interview process, giving the applicants opportunity to discuss their performance (formally and informally) throughout the day, as well as enabling the assessment team to see how candidates reflect and refine their performances, and gain an insight into their metacognitive abilities and their management of the demands of the day.

At the end of the interview process applicants are assigned a RAG (Red Amber Green) status. RED means the candidate is not ready to join the INT6/1 course and is advised to further develop her/his skills and experience. AMBER denotes that they have potential and may be admitted onto the course — dependent on their situation and whether they have a support network in place that will enable them to develop in line with expectations. Conditions such as proof of working with a mentor, or a probationary period for the course would be imposed, and it would be unlikely that the centre would offer an IIDP and support application to register as a Junior Trainee Interpreter (JTI) with The National Register for Communication Professionals working with Deaf and Deafblind people (NRCPD). A candidate with a GREEN status is offered both a place on the course, and an IIDP, and therefore can apply for JTI registration. This approach enables the assessment centre to signpost applicants who need further development and offers a roadmap for their progression.

The interview panel consists of at least two qualified and experienced MRSLIs, who are also qualified A1 Assessors and/or V1 Internal Verifiers, and who are linked to the development programme as trainers, plus one IIDP adviser, who is a qualified and experienced MRSLI, and who also has A1 and/or V1 qualifications. During the course of the day the IIDP adviser observes the interviews, and liaises with the interviewers on the selection of candidates for the course.

Following the interview, applicants who are offered a place, and who are deemed safe to practice will be approved for an IIDP, and will be referred to the IIDP advisor who prepares a report for each applicant according to NRCPD guidelines, which will allow the student to register as a JTI. Applicants, who are offered a place on the development programme, but who have been advised that they are not yet safe to practice, will be supported and monitored during the course and will be referred to the IIDP Advisor when they have demonstrated that their skills have reached a level that satisfies the requirements set by Signature.

This process ensures that students on the development course are always advised by assessors as to whether they are deemed safe to practice. No assessment and training centre can police students twenty-four hours a day; however, the INT6/1 development course is structured so that the first and second modules deal with principles of professional practice, and the ethical responsibilities of practitioners. The aim of this is to develop the students' reflective practice, equip them with the tools to analyse the demands of an assignment in line with their skill level, and enable them to select appropriate assignments and avoid any domains within which they are not yet competent to work. In addition to this, we ensure that students who are being supported through IIDP for JTI application are aware of the shared commitment and joint accountability that comes with the sanction that they are safe to practice.

Interview Structure INT6/2

Part 2 of the Signature Level 6 NVQ Diploma in Sign Language Interpreting assesses candidates on their ability to meet the Signature qualification specification and follows the training component of this programme (INT6/1). This is an assessment programme for candidates who already have advanced skills in both English and BSL. This programme assesses theoretical knowledge and the ability to implement efficient interpreting techniques and obtain feedback on work performed. The programme is aimed at those who have already achieved Level 4/6 NVQ in BSL as well as Level 7 competency in the English language.

Applicants for the assessment programme (Level 6 NVQ Diploma in Sign Language Interpreting: Part 2) undergo an intensive two-day assessment. The psychological approach to this phase of their career path is different to that in Part 1 in that the expectation of candidates is that, by presenting themselves as ready to join the INT6/2 assessment programme, they are declaring themselves ready to become MRSLI. The interview days allow the candidates the opportunity to demonstrate a level of competence in line with national standards.

The structure is similar to the Part 1 interviews in that it includes one-way interpreting (BSL into English), two-way interpreting (incorporating a co-interpreted exercise), with written preparation and self-evaluation for both tasks. This is differentiated in several ways. Candidates are required to prepare a ten-minute presentation (which they deliver on the second day). This task is performed in conjunction with another applicant. Each pair interpret each other's presentation, and so have to work together to complete the task. At the end of the second day, the candidates are given an interpreting scenario which contains a set of complex demands, and which presents the interpreter with an ethical dilemma. They are given one week to submit a 500-word abstract discussing the scenario in relation to their own ethical practice. Candidates who are selected to join the NVQ Assessment programme are required to expand their abstract into a 2,500-word essay.

The assessment team meets all of the applicants at the end of the interview process. This enables them to discuss performance, and to explain the requirements of candidates who are admitted to the assessment programme. In order to identify any gaps in knowledge and experience, a series of questions are asked in the final session. Typically:

- What is your definition of interpreter? Please elaborate.
- Are you aware of different modes of interpreting? Please give some examples.
- Are you aware of a 'Code of Conduct'? Can you give me some examples of what the code covers?
- What do you think are the important personal attributes needed to be a good interpreter?
- Finally, why do you want to become an interpreter and why have you chosen this particular training programme?

Development—course content and teaching methods

Course content
> 'Considering the notion of personality traits at the time of interpreter program admission may be relevant at a future point in time, however given that the predictive potential of the range of dimensions that may impact on interpreter aptitude and performance is not fully understood as yet, it would be inappropriate to use formal personality testing in admission screening at this stage. On the other hand, incorporating trait awareness into interpreter training, and building skills such as self-confidence, positive coping skills, assertiveness and resilience, into interpreter education course curricula would most certainly be useful, given the evidence pointing to these aspects of personality being relevant for effective interpreting. Teaching interpreting students and accredited practitioners to better manage anxiety and occupational stress may be conducive to interpreting performance also. In addition, providing appropriate formal support structures within the workplace for interpreting practitioners (e.g. debriefing, supervision, mentoring etc.) may promote emotional well-being and lead to improved competence and performance amongst interpreters.' *(Bontempo and Napier 2009)*

Historically, the NVQ was an assessment only qualification and contained no development. This presented a challenge for students to formally 'learn' or 'develop' their skills prior to entry onto an assessment programme, except in the case when they were studying in an environment which was able to offer job-based learning in the workplace. This gap in provision often resulted in students opting for the academic route to learn and develop their practice before any undergoing assessment to qualify as an interpreter.

In addition, when the NVQ was introduced in 2001, initially it was unclear what the NVQ structure actually entailed. This, coupled with confused expectations of candidates and the fact that the NVQ did not include an aspect of learning and development meant that once on an NVQ course people often felt that they had not learned enough to become a 'competent' interpreter. Over the years most centres realised that a distinction between the NVQ ***development*** process and the NVQ ***assessment*** process was needed, which resulted in many places setting up separate courses often called Pre- or Development courses.

This distinction was reflected in the new QCF (Qualification and Credit Framework) which was introduced in 2010. The QCDA (Qualifications and Curriculum Development Agency) decided to re-structure the framework to include Guided Learning Hours (GLH) to encourage centres to re-structure their courses, the main difference being that credit points would now be added on qualifications.

The Part 1 of the Signature Level 6 NVQ Diploma in Sign Language Interpreting course featured in this paper describes how students are prepared for the assessment component of the programme (Part 2) and is a training programme designed for students who already have advanced knowledge of both English and BSL. The curriculum provides theoretical knowledge and the opportunity to try new interpreting techniques and obtain feedback in a safe environment. Course content is based on the NVQ qualification specification and prepares candidates for the relevant Signature NVQ qualification. The course offers the following modules: professional boundaries and ethics; interpreting dilemmas; how to prepare for and evaluate assignments; processing; working from English into BSL, discourse analysis; working with technology; working from BSL into English; voice coaching; personal and professional development; and interpreter wellbeing.

The team of trainers

The perspectives of fully qualified and experienced interpreters on interpreting development are a crucial part of the course concept described in this paper and the core team of trainers does therefore consist of a pool of MRSLIs, Deaf trainers and a professional voice coach. This diversity adds richness to the programme, and feedback from the students who have taken part in development courses indicates that this is a core strength of this programme. As a training and assessment centre, we feel that it is important to constantly update teaching practice and materials in line with the latest developments in the profession. The development of partnerships with key organisations in the field is a vital tool for achieving this.

How to adapt to different learning styles

With every new group of students, the teaching team identifies which methods and approaches best suit the candidates as a group and as individuals. Our aim is to offer the best possible opportunity for students to receive training and undergo assessment, and to encourage them to learn in a way that is a 'best fit' for their needs.

Our model of teaching combines theoretical and academic background knowledge with practice and experience in the field. Schön (1987), for example points out that:

> '. . . in examining the relationship between professional knowledge and professional competence, reflection on practice (on experience) is central to the development of professions (. . .); this artistry cannot be learned through traditional models—it can only be learned through observation of competent practitioners, through practice and reflection. . .'

It is useful to categorise students into different learning styles and to adapt teaching methods to suit each by lecturing, group work, practical tasks, reflective journals, group discussions and mixed Deaf/hearing groups.

Practical experience—Working with students outside the classroom

It was identified that in order to provide a holistic learning and development environment, it was important to establish an effective support structure to enable students to gain interpreting experience through controlled and safe assignments. To this end, the following elements have been introduced to complement the core programmes:

The IIDP Process
A separate IIDP structure is offered alongside classes. Students work with their individual IIDP adviser on their professional development and on any areas they specifically need to improve upon. After the initial IIDP assessment (at INT6/1 interview stage) the IIDP adviser will work with the student to identify areas of development and may recommend specific ways in which this can be achieved, for example specialised workshops, interpreting practice or by getting a mentor. The development plan is discussed and agreed on with a review meeting scheduled for six months' time. This allows the IIDP advisor to check on progress and make further recommendations. At the end of the INT6/1 course (typically around eight months after the initial assessment), the IIDP adviser checks on the progress made by the student and issues a recommendation for the next step. This could be further experience or application for the INT6/2 assessment programme.

Volunteering and Shadowing

Feedback from students on the development courses helps to identify any problems with the learning process. For example, it can be difficult to ensure the practicum required for students to consolidate their learning is in a safe environment. This seems to be more of a challenge for freelance students, and so to meet this need partnerships have been developed with organisations that offer professional interpreting services. This provides students with the opportunity to shadow other interpreters and/or the opportunity to work in a safe environment, thus enabling them to develop their practice through experience of real situations.

Personalisation—how to adjust to individual needs

Establishing a personalised relationship with students as they make their journey towards qualification has proved to have many benefits. It enables trainers to identify individual needs from the outset, and work with the student to meet these in as much as it is possible. For example, trainers may be working with dyslexic students and so will need to make classroom-based work more accessible. To support the development and delivery of the taught courses and assessment programmes, it has been useful to establish a policy of reasonable adjustments that all students are entitled to in accordance with the DDA[2].

It is also important to make sure students can learn at their own pace by structuring part one of the Interpreting Diploma in such a way that there are at least two review meetings with each student throughout the course (mid-term and at the end of the course). This provides space to identify any issues and explore the best avenues for continued career development. This also means that students feel confident with their own

---

2 From 1 October 2010, the Equality Act replaced most of the Disability Discrimination Act (DDA).

pace of achieving the qualification, and when, for example, it is recommended that more skill development is needed in the field before applying for the INT6/2 assessment programme, the student is able to maintain good practice through continued registration via the IIDP process.

Students are encouraged to complete the assessment programme in an initial six-month timeframe, but have the option to be fully supported for the eighteen months Signature allows for portfolio completion. We found it useful to increase the frequency of EV visits to our centre per year to allow for as much flexibility as possible.

Post-certification—how to support fully qualified interpreters

The development programme should reach beyond the stage of becoming eligible to register as MRSLI and a range of specialised workshops aimed specifically at newly-qualified or more experienced interpreters can help facilitate this. Each year all ASLI members need to complete a set number of CPD hours and offering interpreting workshops that have been awarded ASLI CPD credits is a good way of continuing to support former students on their journey in the professional interpreting world.

The authors of this paper also think that contributing to the work of key organisations in the field, such as EFSLI, ASLI and WASLI and awarding bodies such as Signature is a crucial part of constantly developing and delivering best practice in interpreting training. The new developments in the area of Deaf interpreting and translation, training of Deaf assessors & trainers, and the increasing demand to develop collaboration between Deaf and hearing interpreters is another exciting part of the constant striving to develop excellence in training for the interpreting profession.

References

Bontempo, Karen. 2009. "The power of personality: A study of signed language interpreters." Paper presented at the *Supporting Deaf People Online* conference, January 28–31.

Bontempo, Karen & Napier, Jemina. 2009. "Emotional Stability as a predictor of interpreter competence: A consideration in determining aptitude for interpreting." Paper presented at the *Aptitude for Interpreting: Towards Reliable Admission Testing* symposium, Antwerp, Belgium, May 28–29.

Schön, Donald. 1987. *Educating the Reflective Practitioner: Toward a New Design for Teaching and Learning in the Profession.* San Francisco: Jossey-Bass Publishers.

CILT 2011. "CILT Languages Ladder." Accessed January 26. hrrp://www.cilt.org.uk/home/standards_and_qualifications/languages ladder.aspx

Professional recognition for Deaf interpreters in the UK

Christopher Stone, John Walker & Paul Parsons

This paper will document some of the history of Deaf interpreters (DIs) in the UK, with examples given of Deaf people working as translators and interpreters since the seventeenth century. Then the recent process leading towards professional recognition and registration with NRCPD[1], the Deaf Interpreter Consortium and its work to ensure DIs can register on a par with their hearing colleagues will be described. The article concludes by showing how the varied traditional work of DIs has been codified into the current registration system and national standards.

---

[1] The National Registers of Communication Professionals working with Deaf and Deafblind people.

A brief history of DIs

Prior to 2007, Deaf people have often worked as interpreters, translators and language brokers in the community without any protection or rights to remuneration. Although Deaf people have been undertaking this work of in a variety of situations there was only partial recognition of their valuable work (see Collins and Walker, 2006). Deaf people have been able to attain sign language qualifications at a professional level, such as the original Stage III exam (1982–1987), which included some interpreting and translation. At that time, this qualification enabled some DIs to register as partial professionals (registered trainee interpreters), although there was no route for progression to full professional status (Denmark, 2007).

With no route to qualification, this continued the labelling of DIs as 'relays' rather than interpreters; relaying is something that all interpreters do when working from another interpreter rather than the source language and is something we see regularly in the EU and UN, those relaying are still interpreters. This forced segregation continued a perceived status difference between 'hearing' interpreters and DIs. With no further developments from CACDP (the former name of Signature) at that time, DIs found themselves in stasis.

One of the problems DIs faced was the lack of knowledge or understanding of their position historically within the Deaf community and its interfacing with wider society. The first example we can find of a Deaf person rendering sign language to English appears to be that of Matthew Pratt, the husband of Sarah Pratt. Matthew took down a written account of his wife's experiences that she signed in an examination by the Puritan Church. Matthew acted alongside Sarah's hearing sisters during this church examination around 1680 in Weymouth, Massachusetts (Carty, Macready and Sayers, 2009: 309). Interestingly, this also appears to be the earliest record we have of 'hearing' people working as interpreters and so the first example we have of interpreting between Deaf and hearing people actually includes a DI and two interpreters working together; the DI working into written English and the interpreters into spoken English.

By the 18th century, we start to have accounts of Deaf people within the legal system (see Stone and Woll, 2008) and then in 1817 in Glasgow a 'Deaf aide' was used in the trial of Jean Campbell, when the headmaster of Edinburgh Institution for the Deaf and Dumb, Robert Kinniburgh, was unable to understand and be understood (Hay, 2008). From 1928 onwards we begin to have both Deaf and hearing people qualifying under DWEB as welfare workers with this qualification including interpreting (see Simpson, 2007).

Back to the 21st century

The Deaf Interpreter Consortium was formed in 2007 (Signature, 2010) with representation from interested parties wishing to create routes to registration for DIs. The DI Consortium had the following membership:

- Christopher Stone, ASLI
- Helga McGilp, SASLI
- Clark Denmark, UCLan
- Judith Collins, University of Durham
- John Walker, University of Sussex
- Anne-Marie Graham, CiLT
- Trudy Field, NRCPD
- Jim Edwards, Cathy Barnes, Paul Parsons, Signature

and sought to build on previous work by ASLI's Deaf Interpreters' Network (DIN). It had become apparent that, 'the new breed of Deaf interpreters [were] currently paraprofessional due to the lack of qualification routes and regulation.'

(Collins and Walker, 2006:20). Furthermore, although the historic role of interpreters was becoming more well known (Stone, 2009), there was still, 'a critical need to have a theoretical model of the deaf interpreting process . . . [and] training' (Forestal, 2005, 235–258). Although there had been previous publications regarding the use of DIs in the US (Bienvenu and Colonomos, 1990), they tended to only focus on intralingual work and downplay other aspects of DIs work.

Finally in 2005 there was a book chapter published by a Canadian DI who regularly worked between ASL and LSQ, as well as other DI work, and it detailed the complexity of the Deaf interpreter's role in different contexts (Boudreault, 2005). This coupled with the explicit description of interpreting within the NOSI[2] as, 'the process where one spoken or signed language is transferred into another spoken or signed language.' (CiLT, 2006: 11) bought about further momentum to change the status quo. At the 25th anniversary conference of SASLI in 2007 a workshop was dedicated to DIs with contributions from Clark Denmark, John Walker/Judith Collins, Lorna Allsop/Christopher Stone and Robert Adam/Breda Carty/Christopher Stone. Here we saw the monopoly of 'hearing' trained and registered 'BSL/English' interpreters challenged.

A new goal

The DI consortium wanted to capitalise on the emerging evidence and political will to support DIs' training and registration. Our aim was to enable practitioners in these fields to attain formal recognition as professionals on an equal footing with practitioners who are already able to register. Previous work undertaken by the DI consortium had identified three clear areas of DI work that required action:

---

2 National Occupational Standards in Interpreting

- Action 1—two-way interpreting between two sign languages

- Action 2—one way translation/interpreting English text to BSL

- Action 3—intra-lingual modification

This required us to identify the role within each area, the relevant occupational standards, the relevant qualifications needed and the route to NRCPD registration.

Action 1—two-way interpreting between two sign languages
Here the role of the DI is the same as that codified in the NOSI. Signature awards two language qualifications for sign languages indigenous to the UK (BSL and ISL) and there is demand not only for BSL/ISL interpreting but also other sign languages such as ASL. As of the year 2011, the new interpreting qualification has been accredited to the QCF[3] and is available as the Signature Level 6 Diploma in Sign Language Interpreting (INT6). The DI consortium has been influential in the design of the qualification to ensure that DIs are given an equal opportunity to become qualified and gain a route to registration.

The INT6 qualification covers all combinations of languages where one is native (to these islands) and is no longer just BSL and spoken English. Candidates must demonstrate fluency and full modality in the two languages, which means if English is one of the languages reading, writing, listening and speaking, must be demonstrated. This qualification opens up the possibility for sign language to sign language interpreting. Consequently, Deaf people can take INT 6 if they are fluent in

---

3 Qualifications and Credit Framework

at least one sign language native to the UK and another sign language. The qualification is accepted by NRCPD as conferring eligibility to register as MRSLI (as long as they meet other entry criteria). As of July 2011 ten DI candidates are collecting evidence to gain INT6 and are looking to be registered by January 2012.

Action 2—one-way translation/interpreting English text to BSL

Here the role of the Deaf translator (DT) includes rehearsed translation and live sight translation, and although this forms part of the traditional role of the DI (see Stone 2009) this does not neatly fit into the NOSI. ASLI's DIN[4], employers such as RedBee media and Remark! as well as other professionals in the field (including Clara Allardyce, Lesley McGilp, Ann Goldfinch, Robert Adam and Christopher Stone) have worked with Signature to develop a proposed qualification. This qualification is based on aspects of the NOSI and the NOST[5]. Signature has developed a qualification the Signature Level 6 Diploma in Sign Language Translation (TRAN6). The qualification is accepted by NRCPD as conferring eligibility to register as RSLT[6] (as long as they meet other entry criteria). As of July 2011 16 DT candidates are collecting evidence to gain TRAN6 and are looking to be registered by January 2012.

Action 3—intra-lingual modification

As noted above one of the issues facing the DI consortium has been codifying the tradition roles of DI within the UK qualifications framework. Although DIs traditional have undertaken interpreting, translation and language brokering work (and

---

[4] ASLI's Deaf Interpreters Network (DIN)

[5] National Occupational Standards in Translation

[6] Registered Sign Language Translator

there is evidence that spoken and sign language interpreters also engage in a broader spectrum of work than their qualifications evaluate—see CiLT, 2009: 5), these do not neatly fit into current national qualifications and/or occupational standards.

The intra-lingual modification includes: working from BSL to modified BSL, visual frame, hands-on, register adaption, etc., and even International Sign. Signature has under taken an auditing exercise with many different roles being identified with no single underlying skills' set. The publication of National Occupational Standards in Intercultural Working could open up new opportunities for those DIs who only undertake this type of work. Signature will work with the Standards Setting Organisations to make sure the roles and skills of those who work in one signed language are accurately reflected in their research on the use of interlanguage and intercultural skills. Even with this support it is highly unlikely that any qualifications would be considered for International Sign.

Conclusions

Although it has not been an easy journey, with much debate along the way, the DI consortium has been able to support Signature in achieving qualifications with associated occupational standards for DIs either as interpreters between two sign languages, or translators working from English text (static or scrolling) to BSL. Whilst not covering all of the aspects of DIs, we have been able to ensure consistency with other qualifications within the UK. Ideally it may be possible for those DIs with INT6 to take further modules in Deafblind (along with hearing interpreters potentially) and language modification so that all aspects of the historic DI role are addressed.

References

Bienvenu, MJ, and Colonomus, B. (1990). Relay interpreting in the 90s. In: Swabey, L. (ed), Proceedings of 8th National Convention of the Conference of Interpreter Trainers, The Challenge of the 90's: New Standards in Interpreter Education. CIT: http://www.cit-asl.org/members/proceedings/1990/index.html [accessed July 2011].

Boudreault, P. (2005). Deaf Interpreters. In: Janzen, T (ed.), *Topics in Signed Language Interpreting*. Amsterdam: John Benjamins, 323–356.

Carty B., Macready, S. and Sayers, EE. (2009). A Grave and Gracious Woman: Deaf people and Signed Language in Colonial New England. *Sign Language Studies*, 9, 297–323.

CiLT (2006). *National Occupational Standards in Interpreting (revised 2006)*. CiLT: London. http://www.cilt.org.uk/home/standards_and_qualifications/uk_occupational_standards/interpreting.aspx [accessed July 2011].

CiLT (2009). Occupational and functional map. CiLT: London. http://www.cilt.org.uk/home/standards_and_qualifications/occupational_map.aspx [access July 2011].

Collins, J. and Walker, J. (2006). What Is a Deaf Interpreter? In: Locker McKee, R. (ed.), *Proceedings of the Inaugural Conference of the World Association of Sign Language Interpreters*. Coleford: Douglas McLean, 79–90.

Denmark, C. (2007). Paper presented at SASLI 25th Anniversary Conference, 5–6 October 2007, Edinburgh, UK.

Hay, J. (2008). Deaf Interpreters Throughout History. Paper presented at ASLI Conference, 5–6 April 2008, London, UK.

Forestal, E. (2005). The Emerging Professionals: Deaf Interpreters and Their Views and Experiences of Training. In: Marsharck, M/ Peterson, R/Winston E. A./Sapere, P. (eds.), *Sign Language Interpreting and Interpreter Education: Directions for Research and Practice*. Oxford: OUP, 235–258.

Signature (2010). Professional Recognition for Deaf People Who Provide Language Services http://www.signature.org.uk/page.php?content=88 [accessed August 2011].

Simpson, S. (2007). *Advance to an ideal: The fight to raise the standard of communication between Deaf and hearing people*. Edinburgh: Scottish Workshop Publications.

Stone, C. (2009). *Towards a Deaf translation norm*, Washington, D.C: Gallaudet University Press. ISBN 978-15-636-8418-0

Stone, C. and Woll, B. (2008). Dumb O Jemmy and others: Deaf people, interpreters and the London courts in the 18th and 19th centuries, *Sign Language Studies*, 8 (3), 226–240.

I think you're my client, but you think you're my boss!

Helen Gillespie & Caron Wolfenden

Biography

Helen Gillespie is a qualified social worker with a postgraduate MA in social work. Helen is also a project leader with the NDCS[1]. Prior to this Helen worked as a community advocate with Merseyside Fire and Rescue and is also an LLB law graduate. Helen has ten years experience of working with interpreters in a variety of settings, starting at university and throughout her professional career.

Caron Wolfenden (previously Hawkings) is a qualified interpreter with fourteen years experience, currently working full-time with Deafinite Interpreters based in Exeter, Devon. Prior to this Caron worked in London and has worked with 'regular' clients for ten years, the longest single relationship being four years. Caron is also an interpreter trainer with Signamic Ltd and an assessor and mentor.

---

[1] The National Deaf Children's Society

I think you're my client, but you think you're my boss!

Abstract:

Improved access to higher education for the Deaf community has enabled entry to more mainstream professions where the workplace is predominantly staffed by hearing people. The steady increase in the number of Deaf professionals has not only led to new challenges for interpreters working in these settings with regular clients, but also challenges for the Deaf professional working with a team of regular interpreters. This paper will explore some of those challenges.

Introduction

The authors of this paper worked together as a Deaf professional (Helen) and an interpreter (Caron) for four years, usually once a week but sometimes more often. Over that time we built up trust in each other and so felt able to discuss some of the intricacies of our relationship and also to reflect on what constituted good interpreter practice. Inevitably this led to discussions about other Deaf professionals and interpreters and we then questioned whether these discussions were unprofessional. We wanted to explore examples of good working practice without feeling that we were in some way betraying our communities (Deaf and interpreters). Our discussions were wide ranging, encompassing issues such as the Deaf professional's working practice, Deaf perspectives on interpreter practice, interpreter perspectives on Deaf professionals and how to work within a predominantly hearing environment.

We also talked about which interpreter suited Helen's work more, and why might interpreters make certain decisions about their conduct. Why would an interpreter refuse to join Helen and child client who were sitting on the floor in a home visit? We particularly wondered if the interpreter could in some way act as 'advisor' to the Deaf professional around issues linked to mainstream hearing office culture. Had our relationship become mutual mentoring? What were other people doing and why was no one talking about it openly? Were our expectations of each other alike or very different, and how could we improve our ability to work together.

The research
Previous research seemed to cover Deaf professionals in a one-to-one interpreter relationship, termed 'designated interpreter' (Hauser, Finch & Hauser, 2008; Bristol, 2009), however we could not find anything about Deaf professionals who work with a team of regular interpreters—Helen would have up to eight interpreters in a week and Caron regularly worked with the same six Deaf professionals each week. Dr Jules Dickinson had been exploring and presenting on the relationship and experiences of interpreters in office settings since 2005, but there still seemed to be gap of drawing on the experiences of Deaf professionals.

Our research was conducted via an online survey. This had its limitations as we were unable to access views in BSL and it was also very long—some people were unable to complete the survey due to technological constraints. All responses were anonymous and in total we received answers from 16 Deaf professionals and 27 interpreters (see Appendix A for further information). We 'forced' people to make some 'Yes/No' answers, which respondents found difficult, as they wanted to qualify what they had said. However, this helped us with our analysis, which took on board many detailed comments. We know more research needs to be done but hopefully this research will open the door on discussions that need to be had.

Survey Results

How do you select Deaf professional/interpreter—what considerations do you make before accepting/offering the work?

A majority of interpreters (63 per cent) accept the work because they are interested in the profession of the client, personal preferences of a specific domain or to complement professional development. In contrast all the Deaf professionals said it was important interpreters were interested in or appreciated their work and were particularly keen to select interpreters who had more experience or knowledge in their specific domain (arts or social care for example).

Gender matching was not considered to be important by interpreters or Deaf professionals except for specific work. For example, home visits are from our own experience potentially problematic where entering a Muslim household, if the interpreter was male.

Registration with the National Registers of Communication Professionals working with Deaf and Deafblind People (NRCPD) and membership of a professional body were important to interpreters (over 90 per cent said 'Yes' to both questions). In contrast Deaf professionals were not so concerned (58 per cent re NRCPD and 75 per cent re a professional body), which is possibly due to a lack of understanding of the interpreter profession. Alternatively it may not be of importance to Deaf professionals.

Another area that caused a lot of comment was about the physical surroundings for the interpreter. All recognised the need for a seat, good lighting and access to drinks, however as one Deaf professional said:

> 'In my workplace my colleagues regularly come and go and it can be difficult to find a seat for my interpreter and can often feel like playing a game of musical chairs.'

With this in mind, the need raised by interpreters to have some desk space can be difficult, especially in an office where 'hotdesking' is the norm.

In addition several interpreters made comments about the way they were treated:

> 'A greeting smile…costs nothing, but you wouldn't think that given the usual dark looks cast your way. A schedule of the day…(avoids clicked fingers to 'heel' when the person is ready to leave the room)…I personally hate not having a seat and desk…its crap and doesn't show any respect to me (and the other terps) as people or professionals.'

Others mentioned that rapport is important and that whilst interpreters may not like the client, they do need to be professionally amicable and have respect for each other.

Interpreters stressed it is important to have the skills and ability to do the work and have time for planning and preparation, and that this is easier to discuss if the Deaf professional has a good understanding of the interpreting profession:

> 'Those professionals who are aware of both interpreting and human needs are my preference.'

Concerns were also expressed about the current economic climate and how fees may be subject to reduction. Whilst some interpreters said they would negotiate their fee, concern was voiced that Deaf professionals would be forced into a position of employing less qualified interpreters who will accept a lower fee.

Most interpreters accept their work through agencies, or direct from the Deaf professional (including the use of BSL Beam, an online booking service). Deaf professionals book their interpreters in a number of ways, subject to individual preference. One Deaf professional said:

> 'Deaf professionals (should) use BSL Beam as much as possible and stop using agencies as they are a waste of public money and cause additional workload for the Deaf professional.'

How do you prepare for the work?
Interpreters use a range of methods to ensure they are best prepared for the work:

- With the permission of the Deaf professional they will talk with their other interpreters, asking practical questions about issues such as about dress code.

- Some regular teams of interpreters have an interpreter book in the office so they can leave notes for each other (signs used, jargon lists and so on). Others use mini e-groups and all are looking at sharing good and consistent practice.

- Ask the Deaf professional about their work ethos, colleagues in their office, their role and responsibility level.

- Regular interpreters working with a Deaf professional may not need 'daily' preparation. This can be problematic for a new interpreter joining the 'team', as who is responsible for their induction (see comments from Deaf professionals below).

- Practical information requests, e.g. venue, participants, how many meetings in one day, breaks, any travel expected throughout the day etc

- If booked through an agency, most interpreters said they would want direct communication with the client and not rely on the agency for preparation.

The diagram gives a summary of the type of preparation an interpreter needs to feel competent and capable of doing the job:

Deaf professionals are aware that practical information is required prior to the assignment, such as date, time, venue, and a brief synopsis. They also appreciate that the interpreter can arrive slightly earlier on the day to obtain further information if needed. The issue of confidentiality was raised in the survey, with Deaf professionals commenting that they do not always feel comfortable in sharing all the information prior to a booking.

If using an interpreter for the first time one of the Deaf professionals stated that:

> 'Induction programme is set up and followed. Time to observe other interpreters in practice, if possible. Weekly meeting to review progress—opportunities for coaching and mentoring since I am not an interpreter. I would (have in the past) agreed to pay qualified interpreters to mentor interpreters (in school context). CPD set up and review annually as part of the CPD system. CPD—not only for new interpreters, also for interpreters who have been in the organisation for a long time. It is good to have recognised training in their field, also good to encourage interpreters to develop in a personal way that enhances their skills and motivation.'

The above would seem to be ideal, however comments were also made about resources to provide such an induction. In contrast, one Deaf professional said 'I don't provide an induction, is this expected?' which indicates that there are no clear guidelines provided when Deaf professionals book interpreters. Who should be responsible for the induction—the Deaf professional, the interpreter or the booker of the service?

What happens during the assignment?
This part of the survey led to many comments and examples, and a key phrase used repeatedly was 'using professional judgement', a phrase in itself open to individual interpretation. Obviously each Deaf professional and each interpreter is an individual so we looked for commonalities that may help to influence good working practice.

Office banter
Office culture involves chat between colleagues as part of everyday social interaction, this influences team dynamics and in an English-speaking environment Deaf professionals are usually excluded from this hearing social norm. Of the Deaf professional respondents, 89 per cent expected the interpreter to relay overheard conversations, i.e. use their professional judgement to do so:

> 'I expect my interpreter to relay as much as possible.
> I will let them know if I want to know or not. They must judge on the fact if they hear it, then I would have heard it too if I was hearing and must interpret it.'

How does an interpreter know what to relay, balancing relaying what they can hear with interrupting the Deaf professional in their work? Helen's experience is of wanting to know interesting gossip and news but not to be interrupted every few minutes—who is the judge of what is 'interesting'?

All of the interpreters said they would alert the Deaf professional, so that they can hear a conversation, often with a subtle nod in the speaker's direction and thus allowing the client to make a decision on whether they want this interpreted or not. However difficulties were mentioned as interpreters do not always hear what is said. Additionally, how are interpreters to know what is important to the Deaf professional—is it yesterday's *Eastenders*, a colleague announcing they are pregnant, or grievances about a manager?

Team-working
We asked if interpreters felt they were part of a team:

- 75 per cent said they are a team with the Deaf professional

- 70 per cent said they are a team with the other regular interpreters

- 60 per cent said they are part of the workplace team

There were concerns raised by both interpreters and Deaf professionals about the impact an interpreter can have on the Deaf person's career. Both sets of professionals were aware that the interpreter needs to 'integrate' themselves into the specific work culture of the Deaf professional and that an interpreter's action or inaction can have an effect on perceptions of the Deaf professional by their hearing colleagues. If the Deaf professional is using a number of regular interpreters are all of them having different effects? Over half the Deaf professionals expected interpreters to be part of their workplace team, while just under half expected the interpreter to follow their workplace values and ethos. Overall, the general expectation seems to be that interpreters need to blend in and provide access for the Deaf professional, so that they can do their job to the best of their ability. Getting to know each other and the rest of the team would seem to be the key to a good working relationship.

Breaks

Both Deaf professionals and interpreters recognised and understood the need for breaks, however both parties were not always viewed as being flexible about when or how often these should be taken. Working lunches, expectations about staying late, working abroad were all cited as being problematic. Interpreters felt compromised, and worried about their own health and the impact on their profession/other interpreters if they were too flexible. For example, they may embed certain expectations with the Deaf professional that they will always be flexible. Deaf professionals felt frustrated when their work was affected because an interpreter needed a break, and the negative impact this would have on perceptions of them as a professional. One interpreter said:

> 'If a client refuses to collaborate with me with regards to my occupational health then I will cease to accept bookings with them.'

In contrast a Deaf professional said that the interpreter disappeared in the middle of a job for a break, without negotiating with the Deaf professional. Clearly good communication and negotiation is key to a successful relationship.

Culture

Deaf professionals generally expected their interpreters to inform them of hearing cultural norms, and this appears compatible with interpreter expectations:

- Greetings and Goodbyes: most interpreters take their lead from the Deaf professional, be it a nod and hello, to a hug and a kiss. However interpreters recognise hugging a 'client' is not the norm in hearing culture, and may choose to inform the Deaf professional, leaving it to them to decide future greetings.

- Interpreters said they dress to match the workplace—some commented that they had seen co-interpreters in inappropriate dress and that this can be difficult to address. Is the interpreter or the Deaf professional responsible for dealing with this?

- Interpreters struggle with interruptions and turn taking between cultures, and are conscious of clashes, i.e. when an interpreter feels it's not the right time/place to say something. They try to manage the interaction to cause least harm—with a sense of knowing this is not part of their training or Code of Conduct but knowing it feels right to do it!

- 100 per cent of respondents said they expected swearing to be interpreted—although one interpreter said they work with a client who swears but has asked the interpreter not to translate but find another word to use.

- We asked interpreters about 'chatting' and 95 per cent said they would gossip with the Deaf professional, but only 65 per cent would do so with hearing people in the same office. Deaf professionals expected to 'chat' with their interpreter but were more cautious about the interpreter interacting with their hearing colleagues. An interpreter needs good social and interpersonal skills, and needs to be able to manage the fact that they are present, finding the balance with the Deaf professional on social communication in the workplace.

Scapegoat?

Interpreters gave examples of being used as a scapegoat by both Deaf professionals (e.g. blaming the interpreter for the Deaf professionals late attendance at a meeting) and by hearing colleagues (e.g. blaming the interpreter rather than challenging the Deaf professional directly). Ill-feeling stemmed from when an interpreter felt compromised by being used as an excuse, and whilst not minding the odd collusion most did not like being blamed for something that made the interpreter stand out. Deaf professionals did not feel they used interpreters as scapegoats, although Helen described how her own choice of language could give that impression, for example stating that a meeting has to finish 'because I have booked the interpreter until this time', rather than 'because the interpreter has to go.' Subtle sub-texts in discourse can shift responsibility and again by having conversations with each other interpreters and Deaf professionals can resolve some of these issues.

Describe the relationship

Interpreters used words such as friendly, flexible, excellent, collaborative, dynamic to frustrating, love/hate, stressful, demanding. All said the relationship relied on respect and hard work—one quote sums up the perfect relationship:

> . . . excellent. A balance between a significant personal relationship and a balanced professional one.

There was also mention about stress levels of the Deaf professional, with interpreters feeling very stressed when the Deaf professional is stressed. The relationship can also be strained when boundaries slip and the interpreter finds themselves doing other duties like washing up or clearing desks, but overall many become friends and manage to maintain the balance.

Deaf professionals described their relationship with interpreters as ethical, good, normal, positive, relaxed, fabulous, honest, friendly, flexible, professional and dependable, to name a few. All of these words appear to indicate the positive characteristics required for a successful working relationship.

Social occasions

Social settings caused difficulties for interpreters, and the top tips that came out were: not to eat or drink alcohol to excess, a need to blend and socially mingle (especially if two interpreters are booked and you are 'swapping' places). If it is a late night event, ensure two interpreters are booked, sit where you can hear as much as possible, watch out for people the Deaf professional may need to know, have a sense of humour and be prepared for any random conversation.

The main guidance that evolved from the survey was that there needs to be good communication between the Deaf professional and the interpreter, and that there needs to be flexibility. Each relationship is very individual, so issues and concerns need to be addressed on both sides to enhance the work environment.

What happens after—Reflections?

Deaf professionals reflect on how the job has gone and whether the interpreter did or did not do a good job. Only 56 per cent of Deaf professionals said that they knew how to follow a grievance procedure, which seems to tie in with only 60 per cent of interpreters informing clients about the procedures. The survey indicates that before following a grievance procedure, there should be room to try and resolve the issues with the interpreter directly. Interpreters need to ensure that clients know about complaints and grievance procedures.

Interpreters also reflected on the work, and when asked if they felt responsible for their client's career, only 25 per cent said 'No'. Interpreters acknowledged that the Deaf professional is responsible for their work but stressed that perceptions of them are also created by the skills and attitude of the interpreter. This leads us to think about if the interpreter is having an effect on promotional prospects of the Deaf professional.

Most Deaf professionals recognised the need for their interpreters to have CPD through mentoring or supervision (89 per cent). However there was confusion about who is responsible for this, and Deaf professionals questioned if it was their role to give feedback after each job or are they only expected to give feedback if asked? Of the interpreter respondents, 97 per cent have external support, predominantly peer groups, supervision and mentoring. Nearly 80 per cent gave and received feedback with their client, and 70 per cent said they debrief, which implies that interpreters and Deaf professionals are talking, but that they need to do more!

We asked about boundaries, and if this changed over time, and both sets of respondents recognised that this happened and that often they become friends and networked/socialised in the same settings. Of the Deaf professionals 78 per cent felt that they did not find it difficult to maintain professional boundaries, as long as both the Deaf professional and the interpreter 'read from the same page', and know their boundaries socially and professionally. Some interpreters said they may take a break from the Deaf professional for a while, or may have to leave, if they feel they cannot be professional.

To sum up the survey, 100 per cent of Deaf professionals felt that they were in a team with their interpreter, which differs to the 75 per cent of the interpreter respondents. When asked how they refer to each other 89 per cent of Deaf professionals said that their interpreter was their 'Professional Colleague', whilst only 21 per cent of interpreters said the same, 58 per cent stating they refer to the Deaf professional as a client.

Recommendations

Interpreters	Deaf Professionals
Selection	
- Assess own skills—can you do the job - Be registered with the NRCPD - Be member of interpreter professional body - Sample the work before accepting a block booking, i.e. accept one or two assignments - Ensure preparation time with client booked in prior to first interpreting assignment - Ensure equipment in place (e.g. telephone headsets) and you know where you will be sitting - Agree the fee	- Check the qualification level of the interpreter - Ensure interpreter is registered with the NRCPD - Have a pool of interpreters - Consider work surroundings—where will the interpreter sit? - Ensure you have equipment in place, e.g. a telephone headset - Be flexible

Interpreters	Deaf Professionals
Preparation	
- Research— if booked through an agency ask for any relevant information they have, then communicate direct with the Deaf professional - Understand what the Deaf professional wants from meetings/their work – what is their aim? - Get permission from the Deaf professional to liaise with their other regular interpreters - Know the dress code - Find out how other regular interpreters communicate with each other and join in - Make sure you know any travel involved in the job and plan for this - Get an idea of what interpreting will be expected in the day – how many and duration of meetings, planned breaks, who is the co-interpreter (if any) - Decide if the work ethos is one that you can work in—will you fit in?	- Provide an induction package - Trial a new interpreter with one or two bookings - Allow interpreters to communicate with each other for preparation - Ensure all preparation is printed off or provided prior to the booking - As an outcome of discussion at the ASLI Conference 2010, perhaps a standard pro forma should be created to advise all deaf professionals what information is required prior to the booking

I think you're my client, but you think you're my boss!

Interpreters	Deaf Professionals
During	
- Be prepared - Be flexible - Have some ground rules and negotiate - Talk with your client - Consider safety and risk - Take a lead from your client and agree to compromise when difficulties arise	- Treat the interpreter as you would another colleague - Have constant communication with your interpreter - Have some ground rules and negotiate - Don't be afraid to ask - Be flexible—interpreters are human - Consider use of language
Reflection	
- Have some kind of formal support – peer groups, supervision, mentoring - Have discussions with the Deaf professional—how do we expect them to know about our work? - Have good terms and conditions and talk about them - Address areas of concern—do not leave them to fester	- Choose the interpreter in accordance to your profession - Communicate honestly about grievances - Understand complaints and grievance procedures - Negotiate

Conclusion

We hope that this paper will encourage open discussion between Deaf professionals and their interpreting team, influencing interpreter training and enabling interpreters and Deaf people to work together to enhance a positive working environment for all. Whilst we focussed our research on London-based Deaf professionals and interpreters, our findings are applicable to any region. By working together we can make positive changes for the Deaf professional in their chosen mainstream workplace, enhancing their career opportunities and also make going to work an enjoyable and positive experience for both.

Throughout this research we were particularly keen to see how expectations and experiences of both sets of professionals highlighted good examples of working together. We also found examples of when our professional needs clashed or 'collided'. By documenting these we hope to influence perceptions of each other as client or boss so that we can work on achieving an equal and professional, collegiate relationship. We are aware that our survey was limited, and that more collaborative research needs to take place, however we hope that we have gone some way to setting up a toolbox for both interpreters and Deaf professionals to use as well as being of use to interpreter trainers.

Appendix A

Information on survey respondents

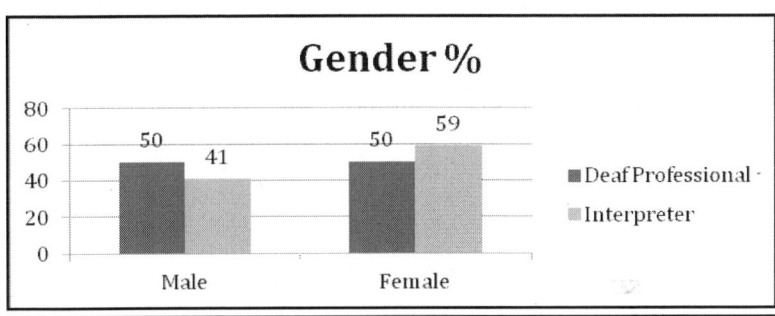

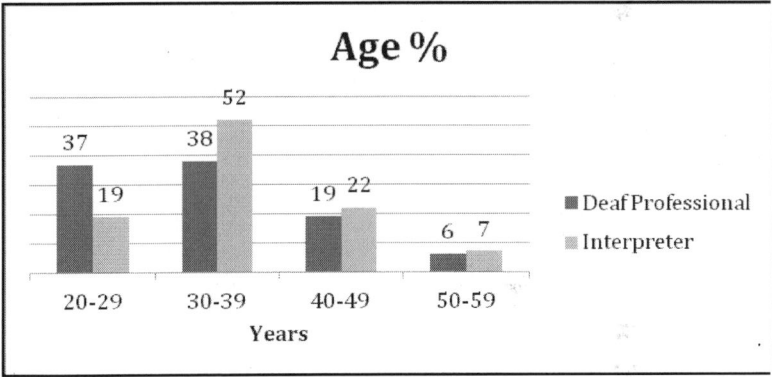

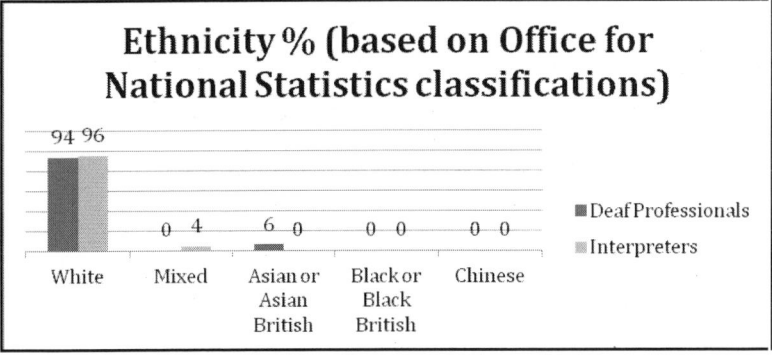

Deaf Profession

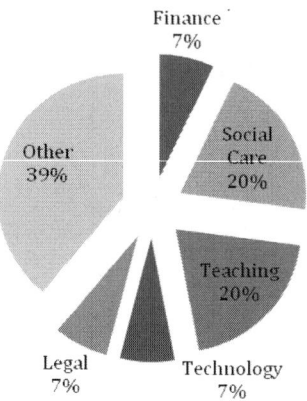

Interpreters—Years Working Post Qualification

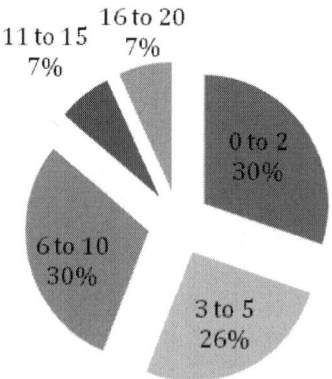

I think you're my client, but you think you're my boss!

Deaf Professionals—Working Years Post Qualification

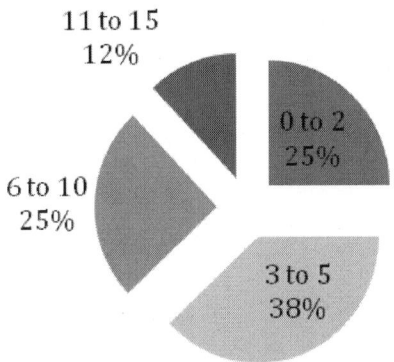

Interpreters—Years Working as an Interpreter

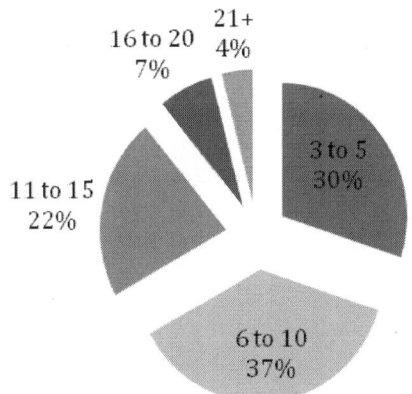

References

Amy Cook, *Neutrality? No Thanks. Can a biased role be an ethical one* (Journal of Interpretation: RID, 2004)

Peter C. Hauser, Karen L. Finch & Angela B. Hauser, eds., *Deaf Professionals and Designated Interpreters* (Gallaudet University Press, 2008)

Simon James Bristoll, *But We Booked an Interpreter* (The Sign Language Translator and Interpreter 3(2): St. Jerome Publishing, 2009)

Jules Dickinson, *Did you have a good weekend? The importance of interpreting small talk in workplace settings* (Paper presented at ASLI Conference, London 2008)

OTHER TITLES ON SIGN LANGUAGE INTERPRETING AND DEAF ISSUES FROM DOUGLAS McLEAN PUBLISHING

Interpreting Interpreting
F Harrington, G H Turner
This book demonstrates current thought and practice within the Sign Language Interpreting profession and is an important reference for students and working interpreters. Two major sections focus on issues relating to the structure of the profession and underlying principles of service provision, and on interpreting practices within health care, education and the law. Informed throughout by the perspectives of a range of Deaf and hearing collaborators, the authors discuss material arising from extensive involvement in the delivery, management and analysis of interpreting services, and draw upon primary research experience.
£20.95 ISBN 978-0946252-48-0 216 x138mm 224 pp

Sign Language Interpreting: Linguistic Coping Strategies
Jemina Napier
This book analyses how sign language interpreters use their translation style and make particular omissions as potential strategies for coping with the linguistic challenges they face when interpreting. Based on a particular study, the findings can also be applied in many different interpreting contexts and the book offers a new way of thinking about interpreting challenges and of how interpreters best meet the needs of their target audience. It also offers a new taxonomy for the analysis of omissions and omission types. Paperback 224 pages
£20.95 ISBN 978-0946252-37-8 216 x138mm 240 pp

Diversity and Community In the Worldwide Sign Language Interpreting Profession. *Cynthia Roy (Ed.)*
The papers in this volume discuss diverse, complex, yet relevant topics that speak to all sign language interpreters as members of communities, nations and areas of the world. The contributions cover the following topics: International Sign, perspectives on educational interpreting interpreter training and international advisors mentoring a survey of compensation for services involvement of the Deaf community in interpreting lexical variation of a sign language a survey of interpreters and their working conditions.
£14.99 ISBN 978-0946252-70-1 216 x138mm 128 pp

Equality Before the Law
Mary Brennan And Richard Brown
The Durham University research project observed court cases involving Deaf people over a three year period, and carried out in-depth interviews with Deaf people and interpreters. This revealed that sign language court interpreters are often not qualified interpreters, or have had no specialist legal interpreting training. The highly skilled task is often poorly understood by other participants in court proceedings, and the difference between BSL and English imposes particular constraints and demands on the interpreter.
£21.95 ISBN (978-0946252-41-1 192 pp

Proceedings of the Inaugural Conference of World Association of Sign Language Interpreters
This book represents some of the many excellent presentations that were offered in Worcester, South Africa in 2005 and offer the reader a sense of the quality of the presentations. Through this publication, WASLI is taking an important step towards enhancing the knowledge and skills of interpreters throughout the world by sharing information gleaned from the inaugural conference.
£14.99 ISBN 978-0946252-63-3 2216 x 1138mm 128 pp

Words in Hand: A Structural Analysis of the Signs of British Sign Language
Mary Brennan, Martin Colville, Lilian K. Lawson
Popular as the classic text for those needing a more academic approach to the structures of British Sign Language. Teachers, interpreters and students will find the painstakingly accurate descriptions and BSL notations invaluable. 224 pages plus charts.
£23.95 ISBN 978-0946252-42-8 227 x 176mm 224 pp

Deaf Identities
Anne Darby & George Taylor
This important title is a collection of inspiring and moving contributions from a wide range of Deaf people that reflect radically changing times. The rising level of awareness of the needs of Deaf people, and the discrimination and oppression they still face, is mirrored by the many changes within the Deaf community. Significantly, the rise in 'mainstreaming' of deaf children, cochlear implantation, political activity for rights and the recognition for BSL, all represent a considerable challenge to the static notion of deafness and deaf people's cultural identity. Deaf Identities is essential reading for all studying or interested in deaf issues, but it is also an enlightening and enjoyable read for anyone.
£21.95 ISBN 978-0-946252-53-4 216 x 138mm 272 pp

Deaf United
Martin Atherton
For at least 130 years Deaf Football has played a key role in the life of the Deaf community, with matches, players and referees a major topic of often passionate discussions at deaf clubs and other places where Deaf people meet. This book contains over 30 fascinating photographs of teams and individuals and traces the history and culture of Deaf football clubs as far back as 1871. Illustrated.
£14.95 ISBN 978-0946252-46-7 216 x 138 mm 136 pp

Deaf Students in Higher Education. Current reseach and practice
Lynne Barnes, Frank Harrington, Jannine Williams, Martin Atherton
No single book currently available in either the U.K. or the U.S. brings together such a blend of theory, research and practice in relation to the support of deaf students in higher education. The range of contributors, their national and international reputations in this field, and the innovative nature of the diverse materials gathered here will ensure this volume's place as an indispensable resource. Focusing predominantly on the U.K., this book will also be relevant to a wider international audience in a field seeking to establish global networks.
£22.50 ISBN 978-0-946252-64-0 216 x 138mm 286 pp

Deaf Studies In Ireland: An Introduction
Patrick McDonnell (Ed.)
This exciting reader marks an important development in Deaf Studies in Ireland. Contributors representing a broad range of research interests have come together for the first time, reflecting new perspectives in Irish Sign Language and the Irish Deaf community. The book urges cultural rather than clinical responses to Deaf experience and identity. It is a useful resource for Deaf Studies students at all levels and the general reader interested in the field. Paperback 208 pages 2004
£21.95 ISBN 978-0946252-57-2 216 x 138mm 208 pp

Deaf Studies Curriculum: Foundation Stage to Key Stage Four for Deaf Children
National Deaf Studies Working Group
The Deaf Studies Curriculum pack is designed to assist children in exploring all aspects of their identity as bilingual children in today's multi-cultural world. Many deaf children arrive at school having had limited or no access to the Deaf community. This curriculum aims to instil pride and a strong sense of identity in Deaf people in society and understanding different modes of communication used by Deaf people.
£99.00 ISBN 978-0946252-68-8 216 x138mm BOOK/CD-ROM Pack

And the Journey Begins
Cyril Axelrod
Created via a combination of sign language, tactile communication and Braille, Fr Cyril Axelrod tells the story of his remarkable life and work. Born profoundly deaf into an Orthodox Jewish hearing family in South Africa, he tells of his early childhood, family life and schooldays, when it was hard to communicate fully with his parents. After a wrenching spiritual journey, he was baptised into the Catholic Church and became a priest. Then, undeterred by a devastating diagnosis of Usher syndrome that has led to his blindness, he continuedto work tirelessly for others in Britain. His work and his love for all people transcend disability, colour, creed and faith. This fascinating story told with remarkable humanity and humour will give inspiration to many and provide an enlightening and enjoyable read for everyone.
£12.95 ISBN 978-0946252-04-1 216 x 138 240 pp

All available at www.forestbookshop.com and from all good bookshops